Table of Contents

* Foreword
* Preface
* Chapter 1: Why Our Healthcare System Is Breaking
* Chapter 2: The $400K Myth: Exposing the Lies About GP Incomes
* Chapter 3: Medicare Reality: Insurance, Not a Free Ticket
* Chapter 4: The Hidden Tax Trap – PSI Rules & Payroll Punishment
* Chapter 5: GPs Are Specialists – The Training You Never See
* Chapter 6: The GP Business Paradox: High Turnover, Low Income
* Chapter 7: The Media and Political Smokescreens
* Chapter 8: GPs: More Than Just Writing Certificates
* Chapter 9: The Silent Tears of General Practice: The Burnout Crisis
* Chapter 10: "When Will You Specialize?"
* Chapter 11: What Happens When the GPs Disappear?
* Chapter 12: When Patients Attack: The Erosion of Respect
* Chapter 13: Doctor of Life
* Final Chapter: The Six-Minute Myth and the Future of Care
* Final Words: A Call for Collective Action

Foreword

Australia has long taken pride in a healthcare system built on fairness and universal access. Medicare, once a shining example of that principle, was built on the promise that no Australian would suffer for lack of care due to financial hardship. This was a bold and compassionate vision. Yet today, the very foundation of that promise – primary care delivered by dedicated General Practitioners – is now fracturing under the weight of neglect.

General Practitioners—doctors who stand alongside you in life's most challenging moments, who decipher your child's first ailments, who guide you through grief, cancer, addiction, and despair – are being driven to the breaking point. Underpaid, overworked, disrespected, and misrepresented, they are waging a silent battle to keep Medicare alive while governments quietly dismantle its core.

This book is more than just observation; it is a desperate call to awareness, a plea for compassion, and an urgent demand for action. This has to be written because silence allows ignorance to fester, and ignorance breeds injustice. It must be written because truth, left unspoken, withers in the shadows. It must be written because Australians deserve to know the reality hidden behind reassuring headlines and political rhetoric. It must be written because if the real story remains untold, the lies will solidify into a false history. It must be written because those who suffer in silence need a voice, and those who fight in isolation must know they are not alone. It must be written because without the courage to expose the cracks, true healing can never begin. It must be written because future generations will ask what we did when we knew – and we must have a clear and honest answer. Our hope is that by the final page, you will not only understand the crisis engulfing primary care but will be moved to demand change before it is too late.

3

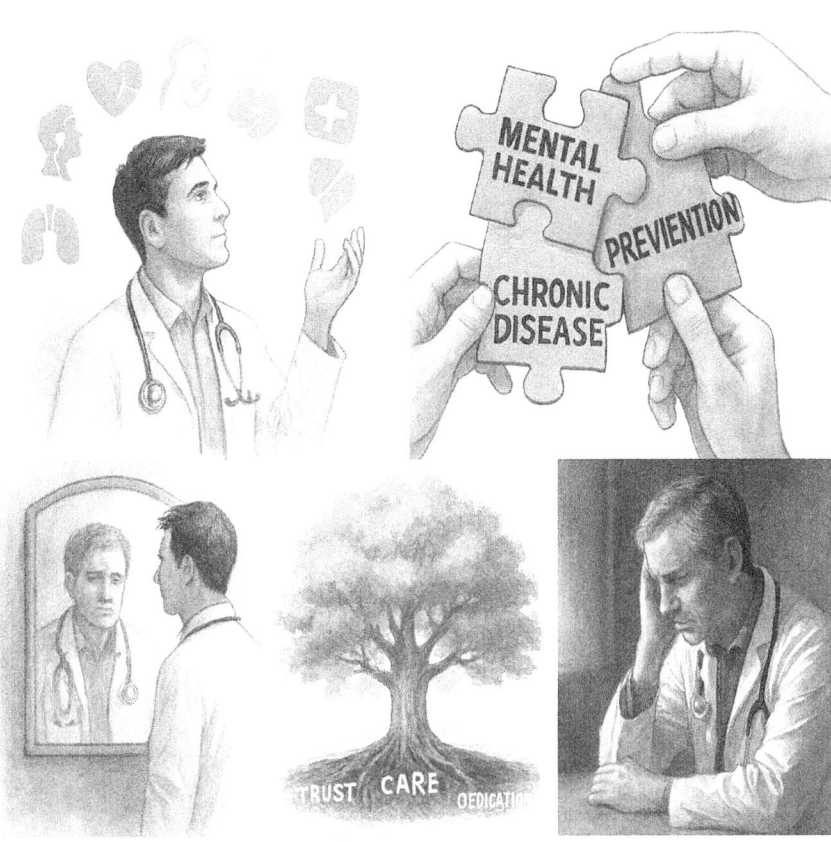

Preface

General practice is rarely a profession of unwavering certainty. Most of us enter each consultation acutely aware of two fundamental truths: medicine is inherently uncertain, and human beings are infinitely complex. Even after more than a decade of rigorous training and countless patient stories etched into our memories, we can misjudge, overlook crucial warning signs, or learn – often through painful experience – that illness rarely adheres strictly to textbook descriptions.

We will never claim that every GP is infallible or that every decision we make is unequivocally right. Like any vocation that grapples with the delicate balance of life, we face moments of profound error and regret: a melanoma missed, a prescription error with serious consequences, a family meeting that unravels despite our best intentions. In these moments, we learn, we apologize, we study with renewed intensity, we seek guidance, and we carry on, humbled by the weight of our responsibility. The truly dedicated among us grow less arrogant with each passing year, not more.
This book is not an attempt to portray General Practitioners as faultless heroes or as the sole guardians of a faltering health system. Instead, it is a raw and honest effort to share, in plain language, the lived reality of standing on the front lines of Australian healthcare today:
* the relentless pressure of hurried decisions and the ever-growing mountain of unfinished paperwork;
* the quiet surge of elation when a life teeters on the brink and is pulled back to safety;
* the bone-deep exhaustion that settles in when misguided policy, inadequate funding, or public misunderstanding needlessly complicate our already demanding work;
* and the stubborn, unwavering hope that, through honest and courageous conversation, primary care can still be salvaged.

If the tone of this book at times feels urgent, even raw, it is because it is drawn directly from lived experience, not academic theory. Its pages reflect the system as we see it daily, with all its inherent flaws, and the future we still believe is within reach – a future where patients, doctors, and policymakers work in concert, not in conflict.

We do not seek to be lauded as indispensable. We ask only that our reality be acknowledged, that our inevitable mistakes be met with fairness and a commitment to learning, and that reforms be shaped by genuinely listening to those who sit across from patients every single day.

What follows is not a plea for elevated status or personal gain. It is a vital record of what we have felt, what we have learned, and what we continue to care deeply about – written with the fervent hope that by reading it, you might come to care too, and demand the change our healthcare system so desperately needs.

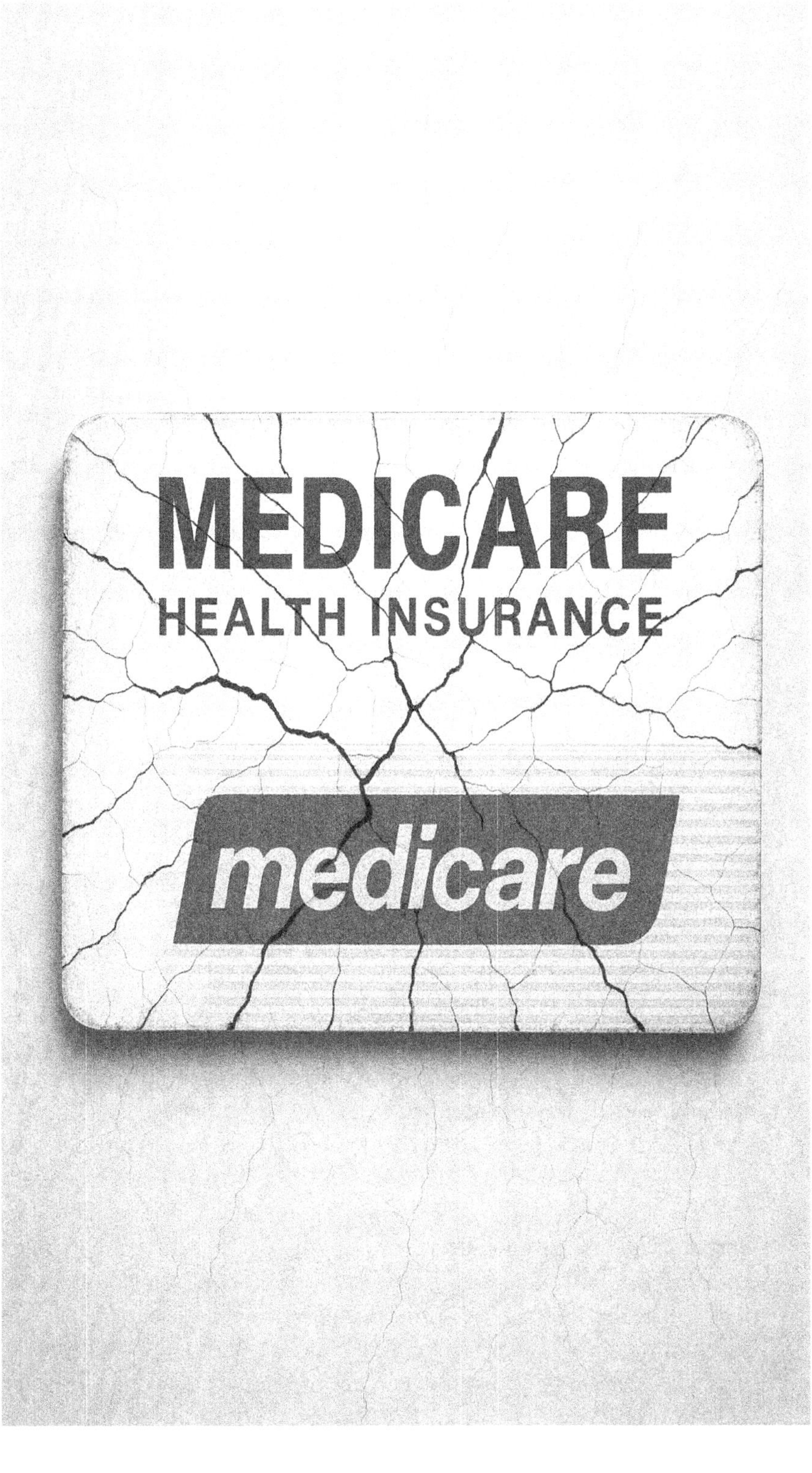
MEDICARE
HEALTH INSURANCE
medicare

Chapter 1: Why Our Healthcare System Is Breaking

Australia has long taken pride in a healthcare system built on fairness and universal access. Medicare, once a shining example of that principle, was built on the promise that no Australian would suffer for lack of care due to financial hardship. This was a bold and compassionate vision – and for decades, it largely held true.
But today, that very promise is slipping through our fingers.

Behind the reassuring political slogans and often misleading media headlines lies a stark and increasingly grim reality that many Australians are only now beginning to confront. Our healthcare system, once a celebrated global model, is steadily crumbling under the crushing weight of chronic underfunding, bureaucratic mismanagement, and a widening chasm between political rhetoric and the harsh realities of frontline practice.

General Practitioners (GPs) – the very bedrock of community healthcare – are facing unprecedented pressures: burnout is rampant, clinics are being forced to close their doors, and skilled doctors are being compelled to walk away from the profession altogether.

The Medicare rebates that are meant to fund essential primary care have been allowed to stagnate, utterly failing to keep pace with the relentless march of inflation, the soaring costs of running a modern medical practice, and the ever-increasing complexity of contemporary medicine. In truth, Medicare has morphed from a guarantor of accessible healthcare into an outdated insurance scheme, woefully inadequate for the demands of the 21st century.
For years, successive governments have obscured the truth behind carefully crafted statistics, selectively quoting gross billings instead of revealing the stark reality of take-home pay, falsely portraying GPs as overpaid villains, and insidiously stoking public resentment against the very professionals who work tirelessly to hold the system together. Meanwhile, the financial and emotional burden on doctors has mounted relentlessly – punitive taxes under the illogical PSI rules, crippling overheads, ever-increasing compliance costs, and the latest

blow: payroll tax being unfairly applied even when GPs are clearly not true employees.

This toxic cocktail of relentless financial pressure, profound professional disrespect, and systemic neglect has placed Australian primary care precariously on the precipice of collapse.

And it is not only the dedicated doctors who are suffering the consequences. Every Australian – every child taking their first breath, every parent seeking reassurance for their worried heart, every elderly citizen relying on trusted guidance – stands to lose immeasurably if the current dangerous trajectory continues unchecked. Longer and longer wait times for appointments, the dwindling number of accessible clinics, the imposition of increasingly unaffordable fees, and entire communities left stranded without access to regular, trusted healthcare are no longer distant threats lurking on the horizon. They are already becoming a harsh reality in many parts of our nation.

Yet, despite these glaring warning signs flashing red across the healthcare landscape, political leaders continue to downplay the urgency with carefully crafted statements. Bureaucrats tinker around the edges with ineffective band-aid solutions. The mainstream media largely ignores the powerful and crucial stories from the frontline. Meanwhile, the Australian public is left confused, dangerously misinformed, and lulled into a false sense of security and complacency.
This book is not a detached analysis; it is an urgent call to action.

Its aim is to forcefully pull back the curtain on the true and precarious state of Australian healthcare, to relentlessly expose the self-serving myths and convenient half-truths that politicians have cynically fed the public for far too long, and to argue passionately and unequivocally for the urgent survival of a system that, if allowed to wither and die, will take generations to rebuild – if it can ever be rebuilt at all.

This is not a self-pitying tale of wealthy doctors complaining about minor inconveniences. It is the stark and urgent story of a nation's health hanging precariously in the balance – and the critical, defining decisions we must summon the courage to make now if we harbor any hope of saving it from irreversible ruin.

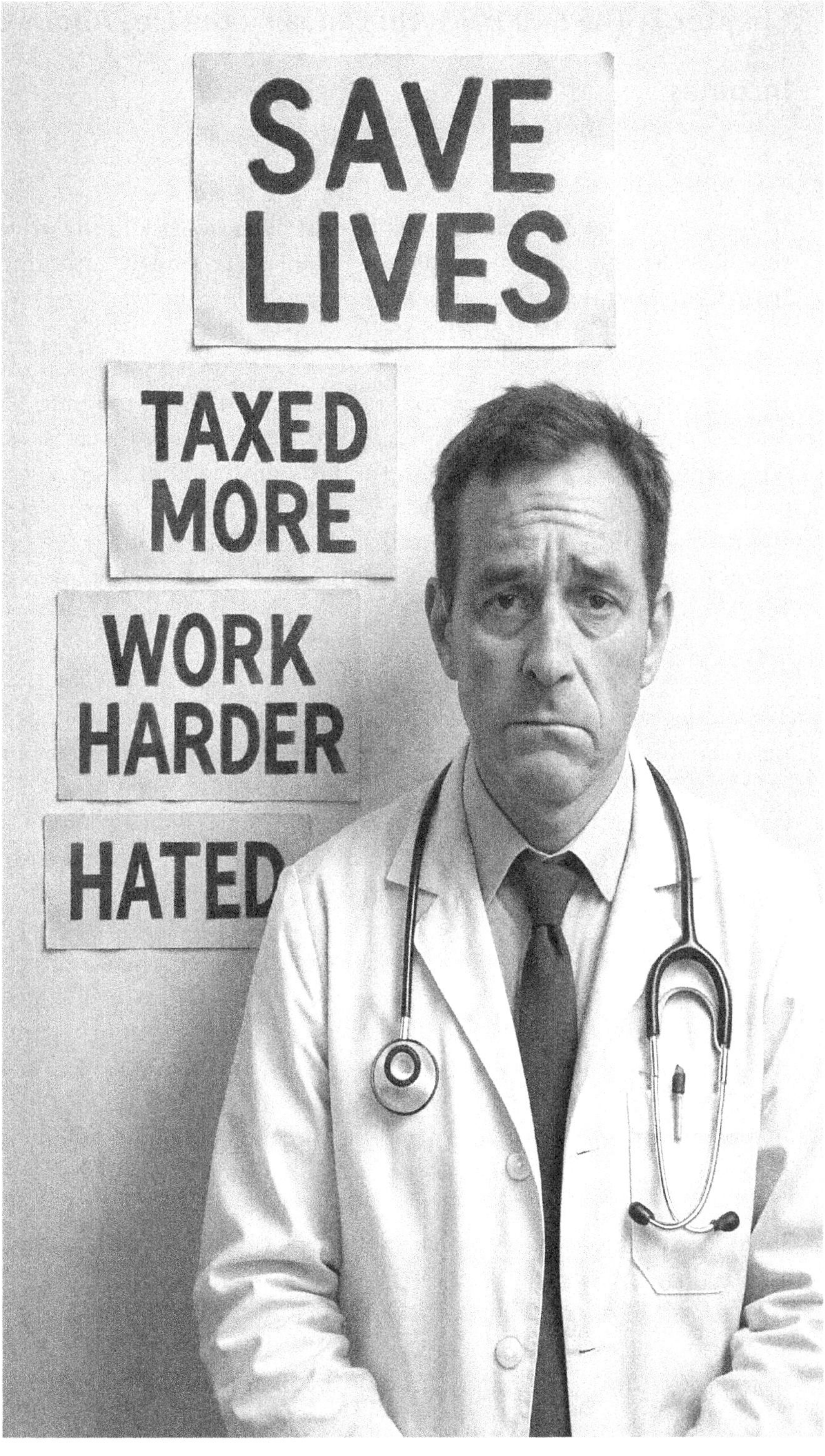
SAVE
LIVES
TAXED
MORE
WORK
HARDER
HATED

Chapter 2: The $400K Myth: Exposing the Lies About GP Incomes

In the carefully crafted narratives of political speeches and the often sensationalized reports of mainstream media, a seemingly authoritative figure is frequently and casually thrown around:
"GPs are raking in $400,000 a year."

It's a sensational headline number deliberately designed to ignite outrage among struggling families, to breed resentment towards those who dedicate their lives to healing, and to paint doctors as greedy profiteers shamelessly exploiting a supposedly "free" healthcare system. It is also a profoundly dishonest distortion of reality – and it is insidiously eroding the very trust and financial sustainability upon which Medicare fundamentally depends.

Let's begin with the unvarnished truth:
The frequently cited "$400k" figure represents gross billings – not the personal income that a GP actually takes home to support their family.

Gross billings are simply the total amount that a GP charges to Medicare (and to patients, if the clinic is forced to impose any out-of-pocket "gap" fees) for the medical services they provide.

It is the top-line revenue figure, calculated before a single essential operating expense is paid: not for the ever-increasing cost of clinic rent, not for the crucial wages of dedicated nurses and receptionists, not for the essential upkeep of vital medical equipment, not for the indispensable IT systems that underpin modern healthcare, not for the myriad compliance costs mandated by bureaucracy, and certainly not for the significant burden of personal and business taxes.

Imagine trying to convince a hardworking café owner that the total amount paid by customers at the register throughout the entire year represents their personal income – without even considering the staggering costs of coffee beans, fresh milk, disposable cups, the wages of their loyal staff, the exorbitant rent for their premises, the ever-rising electricity bills, essential insurance premiums, and the inevitable burden of taxes.

Such a proposition would be rightly deemed utterly absurd. Yet, this is precisely the illogical and misleading way in which many politicians and commentators conveniently choose to portray the earnings of dedicated General Practitioners.

The Real Financial Breakdown

Here is a stark glimpse into what actually happens to the gross billings of a typical, hardworking GP:

* Clinic service fees: A significant 30%–40% is immediately deducted by the clinic to cover the essential costs of rent, administrative staff, reception services, mandatory accreditation processes, indispensable IT infrastructure, and a multitude of other critical business overheads that keep the practice running safely and efficiently.

* Operating expenses: Unlike traditional employees, GPs are responsible for funding their own substantial professional expenses, including increasingly exorbitant medical indemnity insurance, mandatory professional registration fees, the ongoing costs of essential continuing professional development (CPD) to maintain their skills, and the purchase and maintenance of necessary medical equipment.

* Tax: Under the punitive and often illogical Personal Services Income (PSI) rules imposed by the federal government, the vast majority of GPs are unfairly prevented from utilizing standard company structures to manage their income – instead, they are forced to pay the full individual income tax rates, which can climb as high as 47%, in addition to the mandatory Medicare levy.

* No employment benefits: Unlike almost every other profession, GPs are solely responsible for funding their own superannuation to secure their future. They receive absolutely no paid sick leave to cover periods of illness, no paid holiday leave to allow for essential rest and recuperation, and no long service leave to recognize years of dedicated service to the community.

Once all of these substantial and unavoidable deductions are meticulously accounted for, the sensational "$400,000" figure evaporates with alarming speed. The stark reality is that most full-time General Practitioners in Australia take home a net income somewhere in the range of $130,000 to $160,000 per year, after tax, take home net – and this level of income is typically achieved only by working at an unsustainably high pace, often stretching themselves far beyond safe limits.

This actual take-home figure is often comparable to, or even significantly lower than, that of many other professions in Australia that do not require over a decade of rigorous academic study and do not carry the immense daily responsibility of managing critical, often life-and-death, medical
decisions.

Why the Myth Persists!

The persistent propagation of the misleading "$400k" myth serves several convenient – both politically and economically – purposes.

Governments find it politically advantageous when the general public falsely believes that doctors are already wealthy and therefore undeserving of any sympathy or increased financial support. This convenient misconception effectively diverts public attention away from the real and pressing problem: the chronic and systemic underfunding of essential primary care. It also creates a readily available scapegoat to blame when local clinics are forced to start charging modest out-of-pocket "gap" fees or when access to timely and affordable medical services becomes increasingly difficult.

Meanwhile, sections of the mainstream media often find it easier to peddle sensationalized narratives that demonize individuals rather than delve into complex systemic failures. The headline "Rich doctors complaining" is far more likely to generate clicks and stir public outrage than the more accurate but less dramatic "Systemic government neglect threatens the very foundation of national healthcare."

And so, the dangerous myth persists, often unchallenged and firmly entrenched in the minds of many Australians – even as their own access to timely, affordable, and high-quality healthcare quietly but steadily deteriorates.

The Real Consequences

This deliberate and persistent lie does far more than simply tarnish the hard-earned reputation of dedicated and overworked doctors. It directly and significantly contributes to a cascade of negative consequences that are actively undermining our healthcare system:

* Rampant Burnout: Doctors are increasingly forced to work longer and longer hours, managing higher and higher patient loads, all for diminishing financial returns and dwindling professional satisfaction.

* Widespread Clinic Closures: Small medical practices, particularly those located in rural and outer suburban areas where financial margins are already razor-thin, are becoming increasingly financially unsustainable and are being forced to close their doors permanently, leaving entire communities without access to essential care.

* Crippling Workforce Shortages: Fewer and fewer bright young medical graduates are choosing to specialize in general practice, recognizing the unsustainable pressures and the lack of financial and professional recognition, thus exacerbating the looming crisis in primary care workforce numbers.

* Worsening Public Health Outcomes: When communities lose access to consistent and trusted primary care, minor health issues are more likely to escalate into serious emergencies, leading to more preventable hospital admissions, increased suffering, and ultimately poorer public health outcomes for all Australians.

The $400k myth is not a harmless exaggeration or a trivial misunderstanding. It is a dangerous wedge that actively divides communities from their dedicated doctors and significantly accelerates the breakdown of the very healthcare system that every Australian relies upon.

If we are truly serious about preserving the core principles of Medicare and ensuring equitable access to healthcare for all, the first and most crucial step is brutally simple:
Tell the truth.

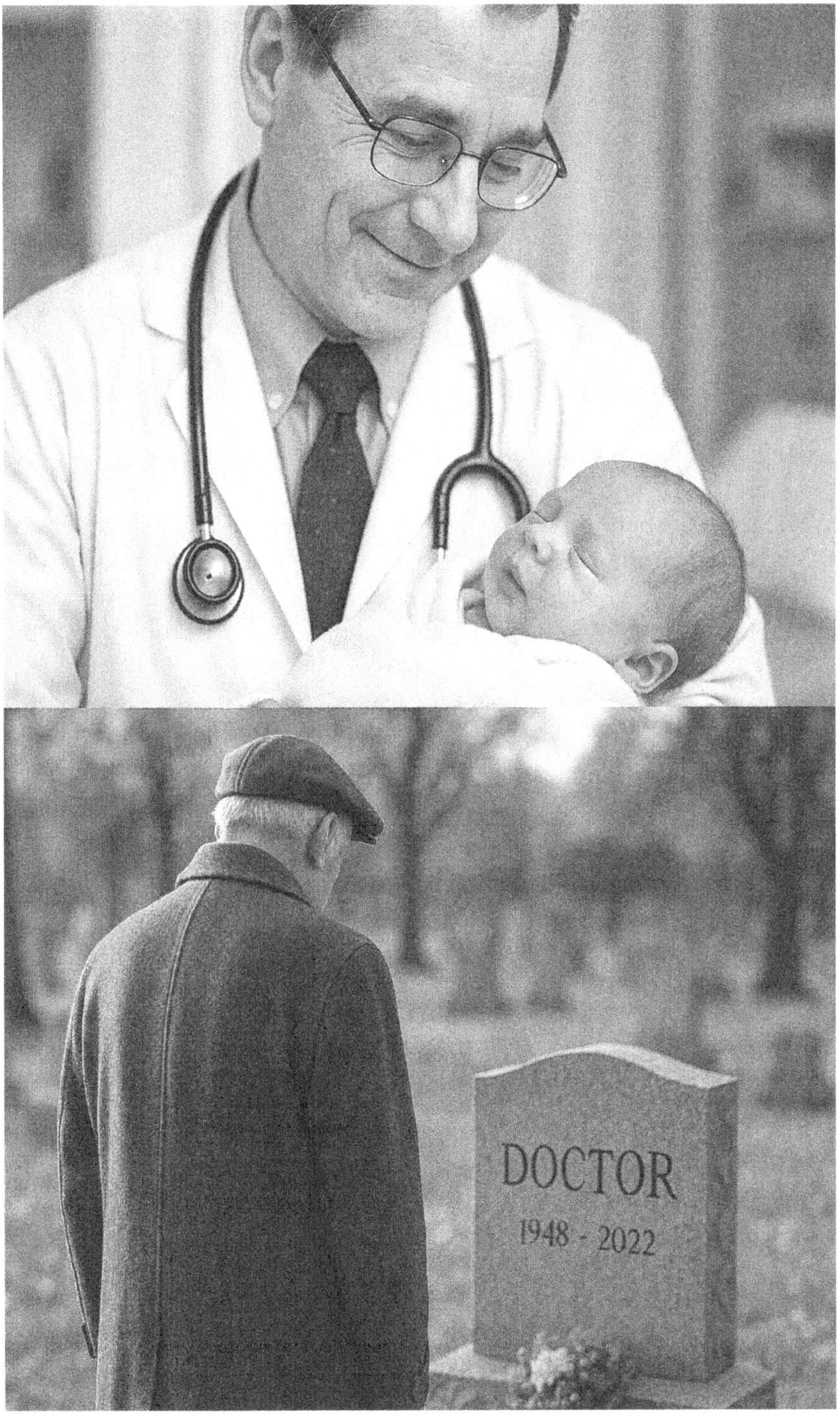
DOCTOR
1948 - 2022

Chapter 3: Medicare Reality is an Insurance, Not a Free Ticket

Australians have grown up with the comforting belief that healthcare in this country is fundamentally "free" – that Medicare acts as an unwavering guarantee of unlimited access to medical professionals without any direct cost to the individual.

It's an appealing idea, deeply ingrained in our national psyche. It's also a dangerously simplistic and ultimately unsustainable myth.

The unvarnished truth is both simpler and far less widely understood: Medicare is not an unlimited, no-strings-attached blank cheque for every conceivable medical service. Instead, it is a public insurance system – carefully designed to subsidize, rather than fully cover, the costs associated with your medical care.

Just like private health insurance policies come with inherent limitations, specific exclusions, and often significant co-payments, Medicare has always operated under the fundamental assumption that it would partially reimburse the costs of medical services – not entirely eliminate them for every individual in every situation.

This crucial distinction matters enormously. Because when the financial reimbursements provided by Medicare – the rebates – fail to keep pace with the ever-increasing realities of the cost of delivering modern healthcare, someone, somewhere, must inevitably absorb the growing financial shortfall. And for far too many years now, that "someone" has been your dedicated General Practitioner.

The Rebate Freeze and Its Devastating Impact Between the years 2012 and 2018, the Australian Government, in a series of shortsighted decisions, implemented a prolonged freeze on Medicare rebates.

This meant that while the general cost of living for all Australians soared relentlessly, and while the actual costs of running a modern medical practice skyrocketed by more than 30%, the fundamental amount that Medicare paid to doctors for each patient consultation did not increase by a single cent.

Even in the years since this damaging freeze was finally lifted, the subsequent increases to Medicare rebates have been minuscule and utterly inadequate – nowhere near enough to even begin to catch up with the relentless surge in real-world expenses faced by medical practices every single day.

In practical terms, this means:

* A standard, basic General Practice consultation (classified as a Level B consult, typically lasting less than 20 minutes) currently attracts a Medicare rebate of approximately $42.85.

* The respected Australian Medical Association (AMA) has consistently recommended that the fair and sustainable value for a standard GP consultation, based on factors such as inflation, the actual time required for quality care, and the increasing complexity of medical issues, should realistically be in the range of $90 to $100.

Medicare, in its current state, covers less than half of the true and fair cost of a standard GP consultation. Yet, patients are often understandably frustrated, and sometimes even outraged, when their local clinic is forced to ask them to pay a modest out-of-pocket "gap" fee – whether it's $20, $30, or even $50 – to help bridge the ever-widening chasm between the inadequate Medicare rebate and the actual cost of providing high-quality medical care.

Why does this frustration and outrage occur?

Largely because the government has consistently failed to clearly communicate to the Australian public that Medicare was fundamentally designed to subsidize, not to fully fund, all aspects of primary medical care. And because successive governments, from both sides of the political spectrum, have found it far more politically expedient to quietly allow dedicated doctors to absorb the ever-increasing financial pressures than to engage in the difficult but necessary public conversations about the critical need for properly funding our national healthcare system.

The Emotional Blackmail of 'Bulk Billing'

The practice of "bulk billing" – where a doctor directly bills Medicare and accepts the government rebate as the full and final payment for their services, charging no additional fee to the patient – has been insidiously weaponized for political gain.

Doctors who continue to bulk bill, often at significant personal and professional cost, are publicly praised as virtuous. Conversely, those who are forced to introduce modest "gap" fees to ensure the financial survival of their practices are often unfairly vilified as greedy and uncaring.

Politicians routinely and proudly boast about "boosting bulk billing rates," conveniently omitting the crucial context that these rates are being maintained on the backs of increasingly financially strained doctors and unsustainable practice models.

It's as if the doctors themselves are somehow to blame when the fundamental economics of providing comprehensive healthcare at current rebate levels become demonstrably impossible.

The stark reality is that bulk billing, at the current, woefully inadequate Medicare rebate levels, is becoming increasingly unviable for any medical clinic that strives to pay its dedicated staff fair wages, maintain safe and hygienic facilities, invest in essential medical equipment and technology, and, most importantly, attract and retain highly skilled and compassionate doctors.

Dedicated General Practitioners are effectively being pressured to subsidize the national Medicare system from their own increasingly depleted pockets – and this is occurring at the direct cost of their own financial well-being, their professional dignity, and, ultimately, their very ability to remain in practice and continue serving their communities at all.

The Insurance Analogy: A Clearer Perspective.

To truly understand the current predicament, consider a simple analogy with private health insurance:

Imagine you hold a basic private health insurance policy.
* You visit a highly skilled medical specialist whose consultation fee is $250.
* Your insurance policy, as expected, reimburses you a portion of that cost, say $100.
* You, in turn, understand and accept that you are responsible for paying the remaining $150 "gap" out of your own pocket.

In this common scenario, nobody accuses the specialist of being greedy or price-gouging. Nobody expects the private health insurer to cover 100% of the cost unless you have specifically paid for a premium, top-tier level of coverage. This arrangement is generally accepted as the norm in a private insurance model.

Yet, when a dedicated General Practitioner, facing woefully inadequate Medicare rebates, is forced to charge a modest $30 or $40 "gap" fee to help cover the actual and ever-increasing costs of providing comprehensive medical care, it often triggers public outrage and accusations of greed.

Why this stark and illogical double standard?

Largely because of the persistent and deeply ingrained myth that Medicare should somehow cover absolutely everything, without any cost to the patient – and the chronic political cowardice that has allowed this unrealistic myth to not only survive but to flourish, even as the very system it describes steadily deteriorates before our eyes.

Who Ultimately Pays When the Gap Widens?

When dedicated General Practitioners can no longer afford to shoulder the ever-increasing financial burden and are forced to move away from purely bulk-billing models:

* Some reluctantly begin charging modest out-of-pocket "gap" fees – often after years of absorbing financial losses themselves.

* Some, disillusioned and financially exhausted, choose to leave the demanding field of general practice entirely, opting for less financially precarious medical specialties or even early retirement.

* Tragically, some are forced to permanently close the doors of their beloved clinics, particularly in already underserved rural and lower socioeconomic areas, leaving entire communities without access to essential primary care.

In this scenario, it is ultimately the patients who suffer the most significant consequences. Communities are left with fewer healthcare options, access to timely medical advice becomes increasingly difficult, and the vital continuity of care – the relationship built on trust and understanding between a patient and their regular GP – is fractured or lost altogether.

Furthermore, the public hospital system – already operating under immense strain and often at overcapacity – becomes even more overwhelmed, as individuals who could have been effectively and affordably treated early on by a community-based GP are forced to seek increasingly delayed and expensive care in emergency departments.

The persistent and unrealistic idea that we can continue to demand "free" and unlimited General Practice services indefinitely while simultaneously refusing to adequately fund the very doctors who provide that care is a dangerous and ultimately self-destructive fantasy. And fantasies, when left unchallenged by reality, inevitably and catastrophically collapse.

RULES

Chapter 4: The Hidden Tax Trap – PSI Rules & Payroll Punishment

Australia frequently champions small business as the vital engine of its economy – yet, when a dedicated General Practitioner attempts to operate their medical clinic with the same financial structures and principles as any other responsible small professional practice, the intricate and often illogical tax system suddenly and punitively changes the rules of the game.

Two distinct and often conflicting tax regimes – the federal Personal Services Income (PSI) rules and the state-based payroll tax – collude to unfairly penalize General Practitioners in a manner that few other professionals in Australia experience.

4.1 What is Personal Services Income?

Under the complex and often counterintuitive Personal Services Income (PSI) rules enacted by the Australian Taxation Office (ATO), if more than 50 percent of your professional revenue is deemed to be derived directly from your own personal labor or specialized expertise – and if you fail to satisfy one of a series of narrowly defined and often difficult-to-meet "business tests" – then the ATO will treat all of that hard-earned income as if it were your personal salary, even if your invoices are legitimately issued through a registered company or trust structure.

* You are unfairly prevented from splitting your income with a spouse or legitimate business partner, even if they actively contribute to the practice.

* You are prohibited from retaining any legitimate business profits within your company structure and benefiting from the standard 25 percent company tax rate, which is available to most other small businesses for reinvestment and growth.

* Instead, you are forced to pay the full marginal individual income tax rate, which can climb as high as 47 percent, in addition to the mandatory Medicare levy, significantly reducing your net earnings.

* Furthermore, many standard and legitimate small business deductions that are readily available to other enterprises are unfairly disallowed under the PSI rules, further increasing the tax burden on GPs.

Example – Dr. Chen
* Dr. Chen diligently bills $420,000 in gross income annually while working tirelessly in a bulk-billing suburban medical clinic, serving a diverse and often vulnerable patient population.

* A standard 35% service fee paid to the clinic to cover essential operating costs leaves Dr. Chen with a gross income of $273,000.

* Legitimate and necessary professional expenses for continuing professional development, mandatory indemnity insurance, and professional registration amount to $20,000, leaving a taxable income of $253,000.

* However, because the ATO unfairly deems Dr. Chen's income to be Personal Services Income, it is treated as personal salary, resulting in a total tax and Medicare levy burden of approximately $96,000.
* This leaves Dr. Chen with a net take-home income of approximately $157,000 per year – roughly equivalent to that of a salaried hospital staff specialist with similar experience, but without any of the crucial employment benefits such as paid sick leave, employer-funded superannuation contributions, or the inherent job security of a public sector role.

*And if you take out another 12% for super, the take home pay further shrinks.

4.2 Payroll Tax: The Other Side of the Squeeze

Compounding the punitive impact of the federal PSI rules, state revenue offices across Australia have begun aggressively auditing medical centers, often retrospectively determining that contracted General Practitioners should be classified as "common-law employees" for payroll tax purposes. Once this often-contested ruling is applied, every single dollar that a contracted GP bills through the medical practice can be hit with an additional state payroll tax, typically ranging from 4 to 6 percent.

* If the medical clinic attempts to absorb this significant additional tax burden, its already razor-thin profitability can vanish entirely, threatening its very survival.

* If the clinic is forced to pass this additional tax liability on to the contracted GPs, their already squeezed take-home pay is further and significantly reduced, potentially making their continued practice financially unsustainable.

* If, in a desperate attempt to remain viable and provide essential services, GPs are forced to increase their fees to offset these punitive taxes, politicians and the media are often quick to unfairly accuse them of "greedy doctor" behavior, further eroding public trust.

4.3 Real-World Impact

The combined impact of these illogical tax regimes is already having devastating consequences on the Australian primary care landscape:

* Widespread Clinic Closures: Numerous previously viable bulk-billing medical centers have been forced to permanently close their doors after being hit with crippling six-figure retrospective payroll tax bills, often dating back several years.

* Significant Workforce Flight: Younger medical doctors, witnessing the financial disincentives and administrative nightmares associated with general practice, are increasingly choosing the relative security and benefits of salaried hospital positions or more lucrative and less administratively burdensome locum agency work.

* Inflation of Gap Fees: Economic modeling has clearly demonstrated that the widespread and aggressive enforcement of payroll tax on GP billings would inevitably add an estimated $15 to $20 to the cost of every standard patient consultation, further increasing the financial burden on patients seeking essential primary care.

4.4 Calls for Reform That Go Nowhere

Numerous professional medical bodies, including the Royal Australian College of General Practitioners (RACGP) and the Australian Medical Association (AMA), have repeatedly and urgently implored the federal Treasury to implement a simple and logical fix: to formally recognize genuine medical contractors as the small business entities they are or, at the very least, to provide a targeted health service tax offset to alleviate this unfair double taxation.

While government Treasury papers have often acknowledged the validity of the problem, these sensible proposals have consistently been shelved under the guise of "further consultation," with no meaningful action ever being taken. Meanwhile, state revenue offices continue their aggressive pursuit of back-payment of payroll tax from already struggling medical practices.

4.5 Why Patients Should Care Deeply

Every punitive tax dollar unfairly extracted from General Practitioners and medical practices is a dollar that cannot be reinvested in enhancing patient care.

This directly translates to:
* The inability to hire an additional much-needed practice nurse to provide better patient support and chronic disease management.
* The postponement or cancellation of the purchase of essential diagnostic equipment, such as an ECG machine, which could facilitate earlier and more accurate diagnoses.
* A reduced capacity for medical practices to continue bulk-billing vulnerable patients
who are already struggling with the rising cost of living.

When established and trusted medical practices are forced to close their doors due to unsustainable tax burdens, governments often respond by funding politically popular "urgent care clinics" at a significantly higher cost per patient presentation – often two to three times the cost of a standard GP visit.

This demonstrates the fundamental fiscal madness of starving essential primary care services, ultimately forcing taxpayers to pay significantly more for fragmented and often less effective care.

4.6 A Sensible Way Forward

To alleviate this illogical and damaging tax burden on essential primary care, the following straightforward steps must be taken urgently:

* Formally Recognize Medical SMEs: Treat genuine General Practitioner contractors as the legitimate small business entities they are, aligning their tax treatment with other comparable professional service providers.

* Align Conflicting Definitions: Cease the illogical practice of simultaneously labeling the same dedicated doctor as "not a genuine business" by the federal ATO while also deeming them a "de facto employee" by state revenue offices for payroll tax purposes.

* Provide Transition Relief: Offer meaningful financial relief and reasonable payment plans for medical clinics facing crippling retrospective payroll tax bills, recognizing the unintended consequences of inconsistent tax interpretations.

* Index GP Rebates Properly: Implement a system of regular and realistic indexation of Medicare GP rebates to ensure that the financial viability of medical practices no longer depends on the unsustainable and potentially unsafe practice of forcing doctors to churn through an excessive number of patients in alarmingly short consultation times.

No healthcare system, no matter how well-intentioned, can afford to over-tax its dedicated family doctors and simultaneously expect its already overburdened hospitals to effectively cope with the inevitable surge in preventable illnesses and emergency presentations that will result from a collapsing primary care network.

YET FOR MY PATIENTS I AM THE DOCTOR OF LIFE.

Chapter 5: GPs Are Specialists – The Training You Never See

When the term "specialist" is used in the context of medicine in Australia, the public imagination often conjures images of highly focused professionals such as cardiologists meticulously examining hearts, dermatologists expertly diagnosing skin conditions, or orthopedic surgeons skillfully repairing broken bones – doctors who dedicate their extensive training to a single, often narrowly defined, system of the human body.

What remains a significant blind spot for many Australians is the crucial understanding that General Practitioners are also highly trained specialists – albeit specialists of a different, and arguably even more demanding, kind.
A dedicated GP is, in essence, a specialist in comprehensive, holistic, and whole-person care – rigorously trained to accurately diagnose, effectively manage, and seamlessly coordinate treatment across virtually every field and subspecialty within the vast spectrum of modern medicine.

The Rigorous Path to Becoming a GP Specialist.

Becoming a specialist General Practitioner in Australia is not a shortcut or an easier option. It is a long, intellectually rigorous, emotionally demanding, and professionally challenging journey that unequivocally rivals the extensive training pathways of any other recognized medical specialty.

The typical and highly competitive training pathway to becoming a specialist GP involves:

* Undergraduate Degree (3–4 years):

* Often a Bachelor of Medical Science, Biomedical Science, or Health Sciences, providing a foundational understanding of the human body and disease processes.

* Medical School (4–6 years):

* Either undergraduate-entry or postgraduate medical school, involving intensive learning across the full spectrum of human anatomy, physiology, pathology, pharmacology, and the development of fundamental clinical skills.

* Internship (1 year):

* A mandatory first year of supervised clinical practice involving rotations through various hospital departments, including emergency medicine, general surgery, internal medicine, paediatrics, obstetrics and gynaecology, and psychiatry.

* Residency (1–2 years minimum):

* Further hospital-based experience, often involving rotations across a broader range of medical and surgical specialties to consolidate foundational skills and broaden clinical exposure.

* General Practice Training Program (3–4 years):

* Entry into a highly competitive national selection process administered by the Royal Australian College of General Practitioners (RACGP) or the Australian College of Rural and Remote Medicine (ACRRM).

* Intensive and closely supervised practical experience within accredited General Practice clinics, providing real-world exposure to the complexities of primary care.

* Mandatory additional hospital-based rotations in key areas relevant to general practice, such as paediatrics, mental health, obstetrics and gynaecology, and geriatrics.

* Formal educational requirements, including attendance at numerous workshops, successful completion of rigorous theoretical and practical examinations, and often the completion of research projects.

* Fellowship Examinations:

* Candidates must successfully pass comprehensive and challenging written and clinical examinations administered by either the RACGP or ACRRM, which rigorously assess their knowledge, clinical reasoning, and practical skills across the entire breadth of general practice. These examinations are widely recognized as being on par with the board certification examinations of other medical specialties in terms of their breadth and difficulty.

* Award of Fellowship:

* Upon successful completion of all training requirements and the challenging fellowship examinations, the doctor is awarded the prestigious Fellowship of the RACGP (FRACGP) or the Fellowship of ACRRM (FACRRM), formally recognizing General Practice as a distinct and highly valued medical specialty in its own right.

Total Training Time:

The minimum total training time required to become a fully qualified specialist General Practitioner in Australia is at least 10 to 14 years from the commencement of university studies. This significant investment of time and effort underscores the depth of knowledge and the breadth of skills required to excel in this demanding field.

The Crucial Breadth of GP Expertise.

While a highly skilled orthopaedic surgeon may focus their expertise solely on the intricate workings of bones and joints, a competent General Practitioner must be expertly trained to effectively and simultaneously manage a vast array of medical conditions affecting all parts of the human body and mind, including:

* Mental Health: Effectively diagnosing and managing conditions such as depression, anxiety disorders, schizophrenia, bipolar disorder, and providing crucial early intervention for a wide range of psychological distress.

* Cardiology: Accurately assessing and managing common cardiac issues such as chest pain, heart failure, hypertension, and arrhythmias, and knowing when urgent specialist referral is required.

* Endocrinology: Diagnosing and managing prevalent endocrine disorders such as diabetes mellitus, thyroid disease, and hormonal imbalances across all age groups.

* Paediatrics: Expertly managing a wide spectrum of childhood illnesses, from common infections to developmental delays and complex chronic conditions.

* Obstetrics and Gynaecology: Providing essential antenatal care, postnatal support, and managing common gynaecological conditions.

* Dermatology: Performing comprehensive skin cancer checks, diagnosing and treating a wide range of skin rashes, infections, and wounds.

* Palliative Care: Providing compassionate end-of-life planning, effective symptom management, and crucial emotional support for both patients and their families during their most vulnerable moments.

* Emergency and Acute Care: Skillfully assessing and managing acute injuries, responding to urgent medical assessments such as severe infections and allergic reactions, often in situations without immediate hospital backup.

* Preventive Health: Proactively administering essential immunizations, organizing crucial population-based screening tests, and delivering vital health education to promote wellness and prevent future illness.

* Chronic Disease Management: Coordinating comprehensive care for prevalent long-term conditions such as chronic obstructive pulmonary disease (COPD), asthma, various forms of arthritis, and other complex chronic illnesses.

Crucially, General Practitioners must often perform this incredibly broad range of tasks and make critical diagnostic and management decisions often without the luxury of extended appointment times, access to expensive and readily available diagnostic tests, or immediate backup from hospital-based specialists.

A GP's specialized training is not solely focused on achieving deep expertise within a narrow field; it is fundamentally about achieving a remarkable breadth of knowledge, exercising sound clinical judgment across a vast range of conditions, and demonstrating exceptional adaptability in the face of complex and often rapidly evolving clinical situations.

They are expected to astutely identify when a seemingly minor symptom may be the harbinger of a serious or life-threatening condition – often within the constraints of a brief 10- or 15-minute consultation – and to initiate appropriate and timely interventions to prevent significant harm.

GPs: The Ultimate Specialists in Complexity

The daily work of a General Practitioner is far from simple or routine. It is arguably the most intellectually complex specialty within modern medicine.

In a single morning, a dedicated GP might be required to:

* Skillfully diagnose an early-stage melanoma on the back of a busy construction worker during a routine skin check.
* Develop and implement a comprehensive mental health care plan for a teenager struggling with suicidal ideation.

* Accurately diagnose and initiate treatment for a toddler suffering from pneumonia.

* Carefully review and adjust the complex medication regimen of a frail elderly woman managing multiple chronic conditions, including diabetes.

* Provide sensitive and informative counseling to a pregnant woman regarding genetic testing options.

* Competently manage the emergency wound care of a patient who has sustained a significant laceration

Each of these seemingly disparate cases demands an instantaneous and seamless switching of cognitive focus, a rapid recall of a vast body of medical knowledge, a deep wellspring of empathy, and the capacity for decisive and often time-critical decision-making – all while considering the patient's age, social context, and individual circumstances.

No other medical specialty routinely demands this extraordinary combination of breadth of knowledge, speed of accurate assessment, clinical precision across diverse fields, and profound human compassion within the often-constrained environment of primary care.

Recognition – Long Overdue

Despite the undeniable complexity and critical importance of their work, General Practitioners are still too often treated – both politically and within broader societal perceptions – as somehow "lesser" doctors when compared to their colleagues in other, more narrowly defined specialties.

This perception is not only demonstrably inaccurate and deeply disrespectful. It also has tangible negative consequences, contributing to inadequate funding, policy neglect, and the growing workforce crisis within primary care. It is a direct insult to every dedicated GP who has invested more than a decade of their life in mastering the intricate art and science of comprehensive medical care.

The Royal Australian College of General Practitioners (RACGP) fought tirelessly for – and ultimately achieved – official recognition of General Practice as a distinct and highly valued medical specialty decades ago.

However, public understanding and appreciation of this fact still significantly lags behind the professional reality.

It is long past time that we collectively corrected this damaging and inaccurate misconception.

Because without the dedicated expertise of General Practitioners – the ultimate specialists in understanding the whole human story within the context of health and illness – the entire Australian healthcare system, from prevention to acute care, would inevitably crumble.

Recognizing their true value is not just a matter of fairness; it is a fundamental necessity for the health and well-being of the entire nation.

Chapter 6: Public Hospital Doctors vs General Practitioners

The Hidden Divide

Within Australia's healthcare landscape, both public hospital doctors and community-based General Practitioners (GPs) fulfill indispensable and critically important roles in safeguarding the health and well-being of the population.

Yet, the vast majority of individuals outside the medical profession possess only a superficial understanding of the profound differences that exist in their fundamental financial realities, their day-to-day working conditions, and the very models that underpin their funding and support.

The stark contrast between these two essential arms of the healthcare system is significant – and it provides crucial context for understanding why General Practice is currently facing an unprecedented crisis, teetering on the brink of collapse, while public hospital systems, despite their own well-documented pressures and challenges, have generally maintained a relative degree of stability.

How Public Hospital Doctors Are Paid and Supported.

Public hospital doctors in Australia – encompassing interns just beginning their careers, experienced residents, specialized registrars, and senior consultant physicians – are directly employed by the respective State or Territory Government health services.

Their fundamental funding and support model typically looks like this:

* Fixed Salary: Doctors are remunerated through a regular and predictable salary, determined by established industrial awards or enterprise bargaining agreements that recognize their experience and level of responsibility.

* Guaranteed Income: Regardless of the specific number of patients they see on any given day or the inherent complexity of the medical cases they manage, their base income remains consistent and predictable.

* Comprehensive Employment Benefits: Public hospital doctors typically receive a robust package of employment benefits, including:

* Superannuation Contributions: Employers contribute a significant percentage of their salary (usually ranging from 10 to 12%) towards their retirement savings.

* Paid Sick Leave: They are entitled to paid time off work when they are ill, ensuring financial security during periods of personal illness.

* Paid Annual Leave: They receive several weeks of paid vacation each year, allowing for essential rest and personal time.

* Paid Maternity/Paternity Leave: They are entitled to paid leave to care for newborns or newly adopted children.

* Paid Study Leave: They often receive paid time off and financial support for essential continuing professional development and further education.

* Salary Packaging Options: They often have access to salary packaging arrangements, which can reduce their overall taxable income.

* Protected Working Hours and Overtime Pay, Most public hospital doctors benefit from regulations designed to ensure safe working hours, and they are typically compensated with penalty rates for any overtime worked, including weekends and night shifts.

* Strong Industrial Protection, Hospital doctors are often represented by powerful unions and benefit from collective bargaining agreements that actively advocate for regular wage increases and improved working conditions.

Add-Benefits are
- Superannuation contributions (usually 10–12%)
- Paid sick leave

- Paid annual leave
- Paid maternity/paternity leave
- Paid study leave
- Salary packaging options (to reduce taxable income)
- Protected hours and overtime pay for out-of-hours work
- Strong industrial representation through unions and awards

How General Practitioners Are Paid and Supported

In stark contrast, General Practitioners in Australia operate as independent contractors – even when they work within established medical clinics. Their fundamental funding and support model is fundamentally different and carries significantly more financial risk and less security:

* No Fixed Salary, GPs are not salaried employees of the government. Their income is derived almost entirely from billing Medicare on a fee-for-service basis – meaning they only generate income when they directly consult with and provide medical care to a patient.

* Gross Billing ≠ Net Income, The gross amount billed to Medicare is not the GP's take-home pay. From this gross income, they must first subtract significant service fees paid to the clinic (typically 30% to 40%) to cover essential operating costs. They are also personally responsible for funding their own substantial professional expenses, including increasingly exorbitant medical indemnity insurance, mandatory professional registration fees, the ongoing costs of essential continuing professional development (CPD), and often the purchase and maintenance of specific medical equipment.

* Absence of Standard Employment Benefits: Unlike their hospital-based colleagues, GPs typically receive none of the standard employment benefits:

* No paid sick leave: Any time taken off work due to illness directly translates to a loss of income.

* No paid annual leave: They do not receive paid time off for holidays or personal leave.

* No employer-funded superannuation: They are solely responsible for saving for their own retirement.
* No paid maternity/paternity leave: Taking time off to care for newborns or newly adopted children results in a direct loss of income.

* No penalty rates for out-of-hours work: There is no additional compensation for working evenings, weekends, or public holidays part from modest increase in some afterhours in form of Medicare rebate

* Significant Business Risks: GPs bear the direct financial risks associated with bad debts (e.g., patients who fail to pay gap fees) and the potential for fluctuating income based on patient numbers and clinic viability.

The Significant Psychological Burden on GPs

Beyond the stark financial disparities, General Practitioners often face a profound and often invisible psychological burden stemming from their unique employment situation:
* Every single patient consultation directly influences their ability to cover their personal and professional expenses.

* Any time taken away from direct patient consultations – whether due to personal illness, family emergencies, or the growing specter of burnout – translates directly into zero income.

* There is constant and often intense pressure to maintain high patient volumes to ensure financial viability – even when the principles of safe and high-quality medical care dictate the need for longer, more comprehensive consultations.

* They are subjected to higher effective tax rates compared to many other small business owners, without the corresponding business deductions or financial protections.

Meanwhile, their colleagues working within the public hospital system benefit from predictable incomes, comprehensive employment protections, and robust industrial representation.

Given these significant disparities, it is hardly surprising that fewer and fewer bright and capable medical graduates are choosing to pursue a career in General Practice. When faced with a clear choice between the relative security and benefits of salaried hospital employment and the relentless financial risk and administrative burden of private practice, the decision for many becomes increasingly obvious.

The Looming Danger Ahead for the Entire System.

If dedicated General Practitioners continue to leave the profession, reduce their clinical hours due to overwhelming burnout, or opt for early retirement as a result of persistent disrespect and financial insecurity, the fundamental healthcare needs of the Australian population will not simply vanish.

Instead, the immense pressure will inevitably shift onto already stretched and often overwhelmed public hospital systems – leading to even longer waiting times in emergency departments, significantly higher overall healthcare costs for taxpayers, and ultimately, poorer public health outcomes for all Australians.

Primary care, delivered by skilled and accessible General Practitioners, is not a discretionary luxury within a functioning society. It is the very foundation upon which a healthy and equitable healthcare system is built.
Without a robust and well-supported network of GPs in the community, the entire healthcare pyramid becomes dangerously unstable and ultimately collapses.

POLITICAL MISLEADING TO TARGET DOCTORS

Chapter 7: The Media and Political Smokescreens

When any complex system begins to exhibit significant cracks and signs of failure, those in positions of leadership and influence often face a critical fork in the road:

They can choose the difficult but ultimately necessary path of honestly confronting the underlying truths and implementing genuine solutions to fix the core problems.

Or, they can opt for the seemingly easier but ultimately damaging strategy of actively distracting the public with carefully crafted half-truths and convenient scapegoats.

In the ongoing and increasingly critical debate surrounding Australia's healthcare system, sadly, far too many influential figures have consistently chosen the latter, more insidious path of deflection and misdirection.

Rather than courageously confronting the genuine and multifaceted issues that are relentlessly threatening the very fabric of primary care – the chronic decay of Medicare rebates, the alarming and growing GP workforce shortages, the punitive and illogical tax traps, and the ever-escalating costs of operating a modern medical practice – many political leaders and certain segments of the mainstream media have actively engaged in a calculated campaign of misdirection and blame-shifting.

They have deliberately crafted a misleading narrative that unfairly paints dedicated doctors, particularly General Practitioners, as being somehow part of the problem, rather than the increasingly exhausted and demoralized victims of a fundamentally broken system.

This deliberate distortion of reality serves to erode public trust in their doctors, fuels unwarranted resentment within the community, and ultimately delays the urgent and comprehensive reforms that Australia desperately needs to safeguard its healthcare future.

Tactic 1: The Calculated Focus on Gross Billings.

As has been thoroughly explained in earlier chapters, the constant and often sensationalized reference to inflated "$400k GP incomes" is nothing more than a carefully orchestrated act of political sleight of hand. It is a cynical tactic specifically designed to enrage the general public and effectively distract their attention from the inconvenient truth that:

* Medicare rebates have been allowed to stagnate for far too long, failing to keep pace with even basic inflation, let alone the increasing complexity and cost of delivering modern healthcare.

* Successive governments have, through their inaction and misguided policies, effectively shifted a significant portion of the financial burden of providing essential healthcare directly onto the shoulders of individual doctors and struggling medical practices.

* The stark reality is that the actual take-home pay for the vast majority of hardworking GPs, after deducting significant operating costs, punitive taxes, and accounting for countless unpaid hours, is often closer to a far more modest $130,000 to $160,000 per year after tax – a level of income achieved only through long and often unsustainable working hours, especially after self contributing 12 percent to their super for retirement.

By deliberately focusing public attention on the misleadingly high gross billing figures – and conveniently ignoring the stark reality of net income after all essential expenses, taxes, and unpaid labor are accounted for – politicians can skillfully sidestep uncomfortable and necessary questions about why Medicare rebates have been allowed to become so woefully inadequate in the first place.

Furthermore, sections of the mainstream media, often driven by the pursuit of simple and sensational narratives that generate clicks and viewership, too readily repeat these inflated gross billing figures without conducting any independent investigation into the actual financial realities faced by GPs or providing any crucial context for their interpretation.

The predictable and intended result of this calculated misinformation campaign?

The Australian public is often left with the entirely false impression that their dedicated doctors are already wealthy, greedy, and therefore undeserving of any sympathy or calls for improved funding – when the unvarnished truth is often the complete opposite.

Tactic 2: The Blame Game: Targeting the Individual, Not the System.

When local medical clinics are increasingly forced to begin charging modest out-of-pocket "gap" fees to ensure their financial survival, or when patients express understandable frustration at the growing difficulty in finding a General Practitioner who still bulk bills all patients for all services, the common and predictable response from government officials and certain commentators is to unfairly single out and blame individual doctors.

We hear carefully crafted statements such as:

* "Doctors ultimately have the choice to bulk bill – it is entirely up to them and their individual business decisions."
* "It is the GPs themselves who are choosing to introduce these new fees, not the government or the Medicare system."
* "The vast majority of Australians still have access to bulk billing services."

While these statements may sound superficially reasonable to someone unfamiliar with the underlying economic realities, they represent a textbook example of systemic blame-shifting – a deliberate attempt to deflect responsibility away from fundamental policy failures and onto the very individuals struggling to keep the system afloat.

When the financial reimbursements provided by Medicare rebates no longer even come close to covering the actual and ever-increasing costs of delivering comprehensive and high-quality healthcare, General Practitioners are essentially left with only two increasingly untenable options:

* They can choose to personally absorb the significant and growing financial losses themselves – a path that is demonstrably unsustainable

in the long term and inevitably leads to widespread burnout, clinic closures, and doctors leaving the profession.

* Or, they can reluctantly introduce modest out-of-pocket "gap" fees for some or all patients to ensure the basic financial viability of their practices and their ability to continue providing essential medical services to their communities.

To then unfairly blame individual doctors for making difficult financial decisions in response to a structural funding shortfall is not only profoundly dishonest and deeply unfair; it also actively undermines the very foundation of trust between patients and their doctors.

It is the healthcare equivalent of systematically underfunding public schools for years and then unfairly blaming dedicated teachers when students' academic performance begins to decline.

The fundamental responsibility for the failure lies with the system, not with the frontline workers desperately trying to make a broken system function.

Tactic 3: The Selective Reporting of "Record Healthcare Spending"

Governments frequently and proudly announce "record levels of investment" in the Australian healthcare system. While headline figures may appear impressive at first glance, a closer examination often reveals a far more nuanced and concerning reality.

What these self-congratulatory announcements often conveniently fail to highlight is that:

* A significant proportion of any new funding allocated to the "healthcare system" is often specifically directed towards hospitals, aged care facilities, and targeted mental health initiatives – with little to no meaningful increase in the fundamental Medicare rebates that underpin essential General Practice services.

* The simple reality of inflation alone would inevitably lead to "record spending" in absolute dollar terms over time, even if the real level of per-person funding for essential primary care has actually stagnated or

even shrunk in real terms when adjusted for rising costs and increasing demand.

* When the actual level of government funding for primary care is carefully measured against the overall growth of the Australian economy (GDP) and the ever-increasing demand for healthcare services from an aging and growing population, the proportion of healthcare spending allocated to essential General Practice has, in fact, steadily shrunk in real terms over the past decade.

This carefully orchestrated tactic of selectively quoting impressive-sounding total spending figures creates a misleading illusion of government generosity and robust investment in healthcare, while effectively disguising the chronic and deeply damaging underinvestment in the foundational layer of that very system: community-based General Practice.

The Dangerous and Far-Reaching Impact of the Smokescreens.

These deliberate and persistent distortions of reality have profound and increasingly damaging
consequences for the entire Australian healthcare landscape:

* Public anger and frustration are tragically misdirected towards dedicated doctors who are struggling to keep the system afloat, rather than being focused on the policymakers whose chronic inaction and misguided policies are the root cause of the crisis.

* The vital foundation of trust between patients and their doctors is steadily eroded, as patients understandably feel resentful about having to pay out-of-pocket "gap" fees without a clear understanding of the fundamental reasons why these fees have become increasingly necessary for the survival of local clinics.

* Fewer and fewer bright young medical graduates are choosing to specialize in the demanding and increasingly financially unrewarding field of General Practice, significantly worsening the looming and potentially catastrophic shortage of primary care physicians across the nation.

* Ultimately, Australian communities are losing reliable access to affordable, continuous, and holistic primary medical care, leading to poorer health outcomes and increased strain on the more expensive parts of the healthcare system.

The fundamental tragedy of this situation is that the vast majority of dedicated General Practitioners did not choose a career in medicine with the primary goal of accumulating personal wealth.

They were driven by a genuine desire to help their fellow human beings, to alleviate suffering, to heal the sick, and to make a meaningful and positive difference in their communities.

Now, far too many of these dedicated professionals are being driven out of the very profession they once cherished – not due to a lack of skill, compassion, or unwavering commitment to their patients, but as a direct result of relentless systemic sabotage and widespread public misunderstanding fueled by misinformation.

The Long and Difficult Road Back to Truth and Meaningful Reform

The absolutely essential first step towards saving Australia's rapidly deteriorating primary care system is brutally simple, yet requires a level of honesty and courage that has been conspicuously absent from the public discourse for far too long:

Stop deliberately lying to the Australian public.
It is time for political leaders, from all sides of the spectrum, to finally acknowledge and openly admit:

* That the current Medicare system, in its present underfunded state, simply does not fully cover the real and ever-increasing costs of delivering high-quality and comprehensive healthcare in the 21st century.

* That dedicated General Practitioners cannot be expected to sustainably bulk bill all patients for all services at the current inadequate rebate levels without making significant and ultimately unsustainable personal financial sacrifices that threaten the viability of their practices.

* That without a fundamental reinvestment in primary care and a significant increase in Medicare rebates that reflects the true cost of providing care, the practice of universal bulk billing will inevitably wither and die – and with it, the very principle of equitable access to essential medical care for all Australians, regardless of their socioeconomic status.

It is also time for the mainstream media to move beyond simply regurgitating convenient government talking points and instead commit to rigorous and independent reporting of the unvarnished facts:

* What the daily working lives of dedicated General Practitioners actually look like – the long hours, the complex cases, the emotional toll.

* What the true net income of a GP is after all essential operating costs and punitive taxes are accounted for.

* What the devastating consequences of the continued collapse of General Practice will be for every Australian family, every community, and the long-term sustainability of the entire healthcare system.

Until we collectively summon the courage to confront these uncomfortable truths and engage in honest and transparent conversations about the future of healthcare funding in Australia, no meaningful or lasting reform will ever be possible.

And the longer we collectively delay this crucial reckoning, the more profound and irreversible the damage will become – not just to the dedicated doctors who serve on the front lines, but to ourselves, our families, and the long-term health and well-being of our entire nation.

53

Chapter 8: GPs: More Than Just Writing Certificates

For many Australians, their primary interaction with a General Practitioner might involve a relatively brief consultation for a common ailment – a viral infection, a minor injury, or perhaps the renewal of a prescription for a well-managed chronic condition.

These fleeting encounters can, unfortunately, contribute to a dangerously simplistic and profoundly inaccurate perception of the true scope and complexity of the work that dedicated family doctors perform on a daily basis.

Far too often, the vital and multifaceted role of the GP is reduced in the public imagination to little more than "writing referrals" or "issuing sick certificates" – a perception that is not only deeply dismissive of their extensive training and clinical acumen but also fundamentally misunderstands their crucial position as the linchpin of a functioning healthcare system.

The unvarnished truth is that General Practitioners are highly skilled medical specialists who provide comprehensive, continuous, and coordinated care across the entire lifespan of their patients, managing an astonishingly broad spectrum of physical, psychological, and social health issues – often within the constraints of incredibly short appointment times and with limited access to specialized resources.

A Glimpse into a Typical Day: Beyond the Superficial To truly appreciate the breadth and depth of a GP's daily work, consider a snapshot of the diverse clinical challenges they might encounter in a single, seemingly ordinary, day:

* Mental Health Crises: Providing urgent assessment and initial management for patients experiencing acute anxiety, severe depression, panic attacks, or even suicidal ideation – often acting as the crucial first point of contact for individuals in profound psychological distress.

* Complex Chronic Disease Management: Developing and meticulously coordinating care plans for patients living with multiple and often interacting chronic conditions such as diabetes, heart failure, chronic

obstructive pulmonary disease (COPD), and various forms of arthritis – requiring a deep understanding of complex pharmacology and potential drug interactions.

* Paediatric Emergencies: Rapidly assessing and initiating treatment for acutely unwell infants and children presenting with high fevers, breathing difficulties, severe infections, or unexplained rashes – often requiring swift and accurate diagnosis to prevent serious complications.

* Geriatric Care: Providing comprehensive and compassionate care for frail elderly patients with multiple comorbidities, cognitive decline, mobility issues, and complex social needs – often acting as their primary advocate and coordinating a multidisciplinary team of healthcare providers.

* Cancer Diagnosis and Support: Identifying subtle but concerning symptoms that may indicate the early stages of cancer, initiating urgent investigations and referrals to specialists, and providing ongoing emotional support for patients and their families throughout their cancer journey.

* Pregnancy and Postnatal Care: Providing essential antenatal checks, monitoring the health of both mother and baby, offering crucial advice on breastfeeding and newborn care, and supporting women experiencing postnatal depression or anxiety.

* Pain Management: Assessing and developing individualized management plans for patients suffering from acute and chronic pain conditions, often involving a combination of medication, lifestyle modifications, and referrals to allied health professionals.

* Sexual Health and Contraception: Providing confidential advice and management for a range of sexual health concerns, including screening for sexually transmitted infections and discussing various contraception options.

* Minor Surgical Procedures: Performing a range of minor surgical procedures in the clinic, such as excising skin lesions, draining abscesses, and inserting or removing Implanon devices – often saving patients from having to attend already overburdened hospital outpatient clinics.

* Lifestyle and Preventative Health: Providing vital advice and support to patients on smoking cessation, weight management, healthy eating, and the importance of regular exercise, actively working to prevent the development of chronic diseases.

* Home Visits and Nursing Home Care: For frail and immobile patients, GPs often undertake time-consuming home visits or regular visits to residential aged care facilities, providing essential medical care to those who are unable to attend the clinic.

* Medico-legal Responsibilities: Completing a vast array of medico-legal paperwork, including WorkCover certificates, disability support pension applications, and reports for insurance companies – often a time-consuming but essential part of advocating for their patients' needs.

* Public Health Surveillance: Acting as crucial sentinels for emerging infectious diseases within the community, reporting notifiable conditions to public health authorities and contributing to early outbreak detection and management.

* Coordination of Care: Acting as the central point of contact and coordinating the often fragmented care provided by multiple specialists, allied health professionals, and hospital services – ensuring seamless communication and a holistic approach to the patient's overall well-being.

This list, while extensive, is still not exhaustive. On any given day, a General Practitioner might also be required to:

* Provide immediate care for someone experiencing an acute allergic reaction or a sudden asthma attack.

* Offer compassionate support to a family grappling with a sudden bereavement.

* Counsel a young person struggling with substance abuse.

* Identify and manage the early signs of a stroke or heart attack, initiating crucial time-sensitive interventions.

* Provide culturally sensitive and appropriate care to patients from diverse backgrounds with complex health beliefs and practices.

The Undervalued Skill of Generalism.

The ability to effectively manage this extraordinary breadth of medical conditions, across all age groups and within diverse social contexts, requires a highly specialized and constantly evolving skillset.

General Practitioners are not simply "jacks of all trades, masters of none." They are, in fact, masters of integration – expertly synthesizing information from a vast array of medical disciplines to provide holistic and patient-centered care.

Their expertise lies in their ability to:
* Recognize Patterns: Identifying subtle patterns of symptoms and signs that may indicate underlying serious conditions, even when individual symptoms appear minor or unrelated.

* Prioritize and Manage Risk: Accurately assessing the level of risk in each clinical situation and making timely decisions about when urgent investigations or specialist referrals are required.

* Communicate Effectively: Building strong therapeutic relationships with patients from all walks of life, actively listening to their concerns, and clearly explaining complex medical information in an understandable and empathetic manner.

* Navigate Uncertainty: Making sound clinical judgments in situations where diagnostic certainty may be elusive, and managing patients effectively while awaiting further investigations or specialist input.

* Advocate for Their Patients: Acting as a strong advocate for their patients' needs within a complex and often fragmented healthcare system, ensuring they receive timely and appropriate care.

The Danger of Underestimation

When the crucial and multifaceted role of the General Practitioner is reduced to a caricature of simply "writing certificates," it has several dangerous consequences:

* Devaluation of Primary Care: It fosters a societal perception that General Practice is somehow less complex or less important than other medical specialties, contributing to the chronic underfunding and policy neglect of this essential sector.

* Erosion of Professional Respect: It undermines the professional morale and job satisfaction of dedicated GPs, who often feel their extensive training and expertise are not adequately recognized or valued.

* Misguided Policy Decisions: It leads to ill-informed policy decisions that fail to address the genuine needs and challenges of primary care, often based on a fundamental misunderstanding of the realities of daily practice.

* Increased Strain on the Hospital System: When access to comprehensive and timely primary care deteriorates, more patients inevitably present to already overburdened hospital emergency departments for conditions that could have been effectively managed in the community by a GP.

Time for a Paradigm Shift in Perception.

It is time for a fundamental shift in how the Australian public – and indeed, many policymakers – perceive the vital role of the General Practitioner. They are not simply gatekeepers to the healthcare system or administrative functionaries.

They are highly skilled medical specialists who provide essential, comprehensive, and continuous care that underpins the health and well-being of the entire nation.

Recognizing and valuing their true expertise is not just a matter of professional courtesy; it is a fundamental prerequisite for building a sustainable and equitable healthcare system for all Australians.

Without a thriving and well-supported primary care sector, the entire edifice of our healthcare system is built on an increasingly fragile foundation.

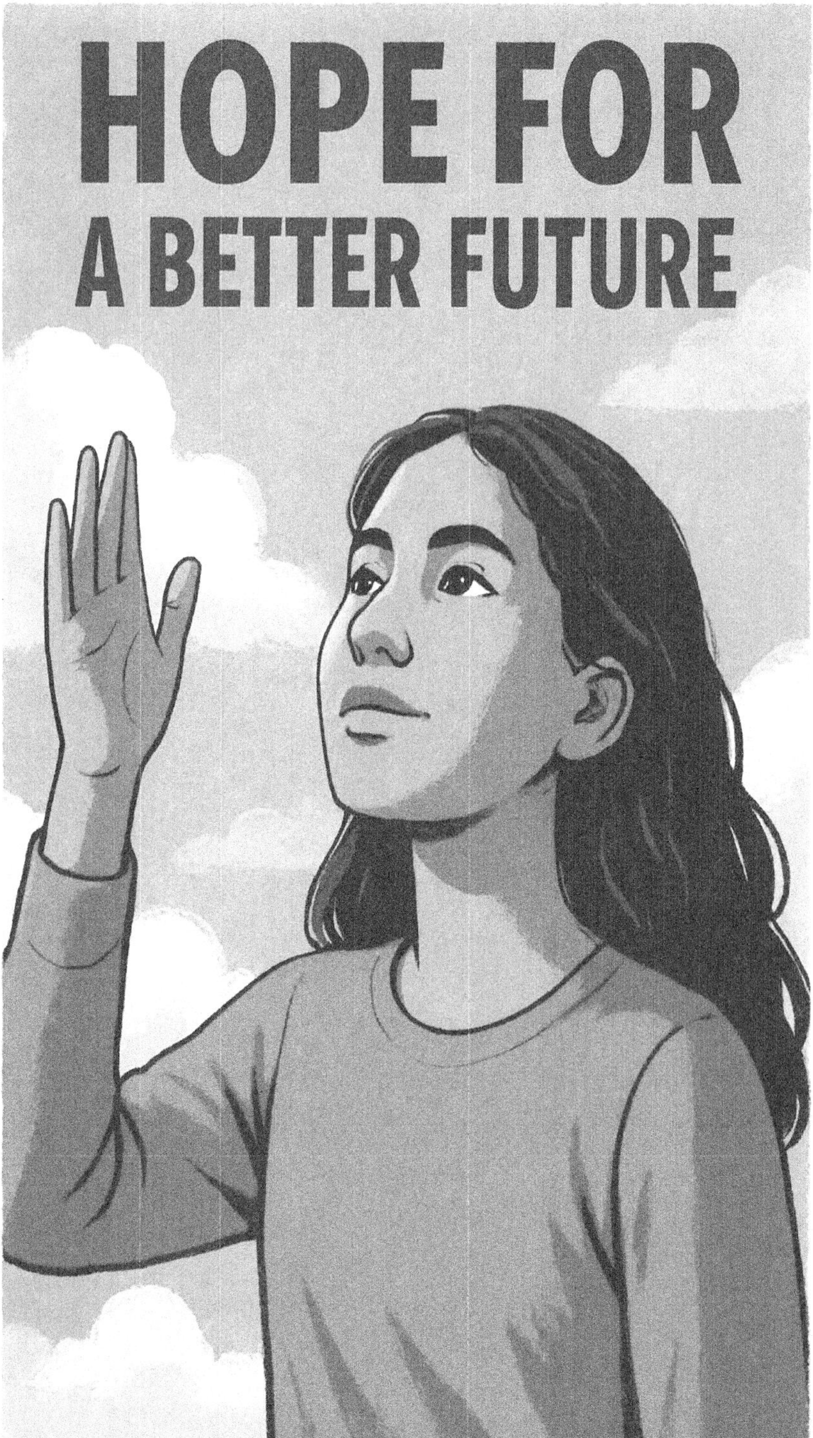
HOPE FOR
A BETTER FUTURE

Chapter 9: The Silent Tears of General Practice

Beyond the often-discussed issues of inadequate funding, bureaucratic burdens, and public misunderstanding, there lies a significant and often unspoken reality within the world of General Practice: the profound emotional toll it takes on the dedicated individuals who choose this demanding vocation.

Every day, General Practitioners step into their consulting rooms and bear witness to the full spectrum of human experience – from the joyous arrival of new life to the profound sorrow of loss, from the resilience of the human spirit in the face of chronic illness to the devastating impact of mental health struggles and social disadvantage. They are the trusted confidantes, the first responders in times of crisis, and the steady anchors in the often-turbulent seas of their patients' lives.

This constant exposure to human suffering, coupled with the immense responsibility of making critical medical decisions – often with limited time and resources – exacts a significant emotional price. While the focus of public discourse often revolves around systemic issues, it is crucial to acknowledge the silent tears shed by countless GPs behind closed doors, the weight of empathy they carry home each night, and the quiet battles they wage against burnout and compassion fatigue.

Bearing Witness to Human Vulnerability.

Day after day, General Practitioners are privileged to share some of the most intimate and vulnerable moments in their patients' lives:
* They hold the hand of a grieving spouse who has just lost their life partner.

* They deliver the difficult news of a serious diagnosis, watching as hope and certainty crumble before their eyes.

* They listen intently to the heartbreaking stories of patients struggling with crippling anxiety, overwhelming depression, or the insidious grip of addiction.

* They witness the devastating impact of poverty, social isolation, and domestic violence on the physical and mental health of their patients.

* They navigate the ethical complexities of end-of-life care, supporting patients and their families through their final journey with dignity and compassion.

* They share in the quiet triumphs of recovery, the relief of a chronic condition finally being managed, and the joy of a new parent holding their healthy baby.

This constant immersion in the raw realities of human existence, while deeply meaningful and often profoundly rewarding, also carries a significant emotional burden. GPs are not immune to the pain and suffering they witness.

They develop deep connections with their regular patients, and their hearts ache when those they care for experience hardship or loss.

The Weight of Responsibility and Decision-Making

With each consultation, General Practitioners carry the immense responsibility of accurately assessing symptoms, making critical diagnostic decisions, and initiating appropriate management plans – often within the space of a brief 10- or 15-minute appointment.

The potential for error, the constant pressure to not miss a subtle but crucial warning sign, and the knowledge that their decisions can have profound and life-altering consequences for their patients can create significant anxiety and stress.

Unlike their hospital-based colleagues who often work within larger teams and have more readily available access to specialist consultation and diagnostic resources, GPs in the community often operate with a greater degree of autonomy and bear the primary responsibility for the vast majority of their patients' care. This can lead to feelings of isolation and an overwhelming sense of being solely responsible for a wide range of complex medical issues.

The Crushing Burden of Time Constraints and Bureaucracy

The relentless pressure to see a high volume of patients in order to maintain the financial viability of their practices – a direct consequence of inadequate Medicare rebates – often forces GPs to work at an unsustainable pace, leaving them feeling rushed, emotionally depleted, and unable to provide the level of care they truly believe their patients deserve.

Compounding this pressure is the ever-increasing mountain of bureaucratic paperwork, mandatory reporting requirements, and complex administrative tasks that consume a significant portion of their working day – time that could otherwise be spent directly caring for patients or attending to their own well-being.

This relentless cycle of overwork, time pressure, and administrative burden significantly contributes to the alarmingly high rates of burnout, depression, and anxiety reported among General Practitioners in Australia.

Many feel trapped in a system that demands more and more while providing less and less support.

The Erosion of Work-Life Balance

The demands of General Practice often extend far beyond scheduled clinic hours.

GPs frequently find themselves:
* Answering urgent phone calls from worried patients after hours.
* Catching up on a backlog of paperwork and referrals late into the evening.
* Feeling the constant mental weight of their patients' complex medical and social issues, even during their precious time off.
* Sacrificing personal time with family and friends due to the unpredictable and often demanding nature of their work.

This erosion of work-life balance takes a significant toll on their personal relationships, their physical health, and their overall well-being, further increasing their vulnerability to burnout and mental health challenges.

The Stigma and Silence

Despite the immense emotional pressures they face, many General Practitioners feel a sense of stigma or reluctance to openly discuss their own struggles with mental health or burnout. They are often expected to be the strong and unwavering caregivers, the pillars of support for their patients and their communities. Admitting to their own vulnerability can feel like a sign of weakness or failure in a profession that often demands a facade of unwavering strength.

This culture of silence can prevent GPs from seeking the help and support they desperately need, further exacerbating their emotional distress and increasing the risk of more serious mental health issues.

The Human Cost of a System Under Strain

The silent tears of General Practice are not just a personal tragedy for the individual doctors who shed them. They are a symptom of a healthcare system under immense and unsustainable strain. When the emotional well-being of our frontline medical professionals is neglected, the quality of care they can provide to their patients inevitably suffers. Burnout leads to decreased empathy, increased errors, and ultimately, a less compassionate and effective healthcare system for everyone.

Recognizing and addressing the emotional toll of General Practice is not a secondary concern; it is a fundamental imperative for the long-term sustainability and effectiveness of our healthcare system. We must foster a culture of support and understanding within the profession, encourage open conversations about mental health and well-being, and implement systemic changes that alleviate the relentless pressures contributing to burnout.

Just as we rightly focus on the physical health needs of our communities, we must also acknowledge and support the emotional health of the dedicated doctors who tirelessly care for us. Their well-being is inextricably linked to the well-being of the nation. The silent tears of General Practice deserve to be seen, acknowledged, and ultimately, dried.

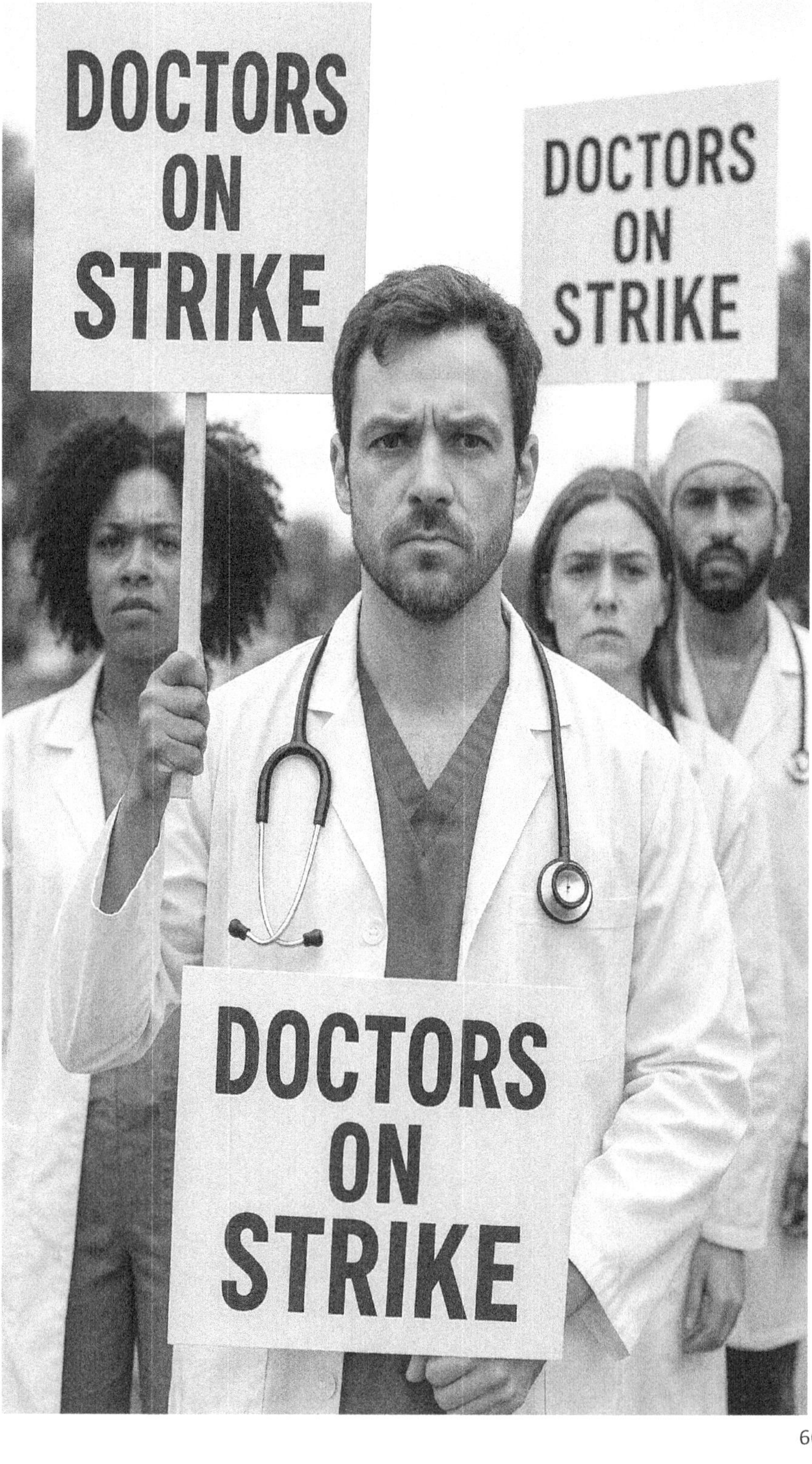
DOCTORS
ON
STRIKE
DOCTORS
ON
STRIKE
DOCTORS
ON
STRIKE

Chapter 10: The Unpaid Hours

Beyond the inadequate Medicare rebates and the punitive tax regimes, there exists another significant and often completely invisible financial contribution made by dedicated General Practitioners to the Australian healthcare system: the vast and largely unacknowledged number of unpaid hours they routinely dedicate to their patients and their practices.

Unlike almost every other profession in Australia, where work performed outside of designated paid hours is either compensated or explicitly limited, General Practitioners are routinely expected to undertake a significant amount of essential work for which they receive absolutely no direct remuneration.

This hidden subsidy, silently absorbed by the Medicare system, represents a substantial but unquantified financial contribution from individual doctors – a contribution that further underscores the chronic underfunding of primary care and the unsustainable pressures placed upon its workforce.

The Invisible Workload: Where the Clock Doesn't Tick (For Pay).

Consider just some of the essential tasks that General Practitioners routinely perform outside of direct, billable patient consultations, often squeezing these tasks into lunch breaks, after hours, or on weekends:

* Reviewing and Actioning Test Results: Carefully scrutinizing often hundreds of pathology and radiology results each week, identifying critical abnormalities, and promptly contacting patients to arrange follow-up care – a process that requires significant clinical judgment and can be incredibly time-consuming.

* Writing Referrals to Specialists and Allied Health Professionals: Crafting detailed and clinically relevant referral letters that accurately summarize the patient's history, presenting problem, and the specific questions for the specialist – a crucial step in ensuring coordinated and effective care.

* Completing Medico-legal Paperwork: Filling out a seemingly endless array of forms for disability support pensions, insurance assessments,

and other medico-legal purposes – essential for their patients but often incredibly time-consuming and uncompensated.

* Liaising with Hospitals and Other Healthcare Providers: Communicating with hospital specialists, allied health professionals, and community nurses to ensure seamless transitions of care and effective coordination of treatment plans.

* Continuing Professional Development (CPD): Dedicating numerous hours each year to mandatory ongoing education, attending workshops, completing online modules, and staying abreast of the latest medical research and guidelines – essential for maintaining their skills and registration but often performed in their own time.

* Practice Management and Administration: For GPs who own or manage their own practices, this can involve significant additional hours spent on staffing issues, financial management, compliance requirements, and ensuring the smooth operation of the clinic.

* Addressing Prescription Queries and Authorizations: Responding to numerous pharmacy requests for clarification or authorization of prescriptions, often requiring careful review of the patient's medical record.

* Reading and Responding to Medical Correspondence: Reviewing and actioning letters and reports received from specialists, hospitals, and other healthcare providers.

The sheer volume of this "invisible workload" is staggering. Many dedicated General Practitioners routinely dedicate an additional 3-8 hours per week – or even more – to these essential tasks, all without receiving any direct financial compensation for their time and expertise.

The Financial Significance of Unpaid Labor

To truly grasp the magnitude of this hidden subsidy, consider a simple thought experiment:
If General Practitioners were to bill even a modest hourly rate for the time they currently dedicate to these essential but uncompensated tasks, the financial implications for the Medicare system would be enormous.

The true cost of delivering comprehensive primary care in Australia is significantly higher than what is currently reflected in the inadequate Medicare rebates. The gap is being silently and personally filled by the unpaid labor of dedicated doctors.

Imagine if nurses, teachers, or other essential professionals were routinely expected to perform a similar volume of crucial work without any remuneration. There would rightly be widespread public outcry and demands for fair compensation. Yet, this expectation has become an ingrained – and largely invisible – norm within the culture of General Practice.

The Unsustainable Nature of This Hidden Subsidy

The reliance on the unpaid labor of General Practitioners is not only inherently unfair and unsustainable in the long term; it also has significant negative consequences for the individuals and the system as a whole:

* Increased Burnout: The sheer volume of work, both paid and unpaid, contributes significantly to the alarmingly high rates of burnout and mental health challenges within the profession.

* Reduced Time for Patient Care: The hours spent on uncompensated administrative tasks directly detract from the time that GPs can dedicate to providing direct patient care, potentially leading to shorter consultation times and reduced quality of care.

* Disincentive for Future Generations: The expectation of significant unpaid work acts as a further disincentive for bright young medical graduates considering a career in General Practice, exacerbating the looming workforce crisis.

* Masking the True Cost of Care: The reliance on unpaid labor artificially deflates the perceived cost of primary care, making it easier for governments to perpetuate the myth that current Medicare rebates are adequate.

The Question: "Are You Planning to Specialize Someday?"

For many General Practitioners, particularly those early in their careers, a surprisingly common question arises from well-meaning family members, friends, and even occasionally, other medical professionals: "So, are you planning to specialize someday?"

This seemingly innocuous inquiry often reveals a fundamental misunderstanding of the depth and breadth of General Practice as a specialty in its own right. It can also feel deeply invalidating to GPs who have consciously and deliberately chosen this demanding and multifaceted field after years of rigorous training.

The underlying assumption behind the question is often that General Practice is merely a stepping stone, a temporary phase before a "real" specialization is pursued. It implies that the skills and knowledge required of a GP are somehow less advanced or less valuable than those of a cardiologist, a neurologist, or a surgeon.

For a GP already grappling with the immense pressures of their daily workload, the emotional toll of their work, and the constant feeling of being undervalued by the system, this question can feel like yet another subtle jab, further reinforcing the societal perception that their chosen specialty is somehow "less than other."

The reality, as has been explored in previous chapters, is that General Practice is a specialization – a specialization in comprehensive, whole-person care across the entire spectrum of medical conditions and the human lifespan.

It requires an extraordinary breadth of knowledge, exceptional diagnostic and clinical reasoning skills, and a deep commitment to building long-term therapeutic relationships with patients within their community.

For a GP who has dedicated over a decade to mastering this complex and demanding field, the question of "specializing someday" often elicits a weary internal response: "I am a specialist. I specialize in understanding the interconnectedness of human health and illness, in providing continuity of care across life's journey, and in navigating the complexities of the healthcare system for my patients. What could be more specialized than that?"

A Call for Recognition of True Value

The unpaid hours silently contributed by General Practitioners represent a significant but unacknowledged subsidy to the Australian healthcare system. This hidden contribution, along with the emotional toll of their work and the persistent societal undervaluation of their expertise, paints a clear picture of a profession under immense and unsustainable pressure.

Recognizing the true value of General Practice – not just in terms of the billable services they provide, but also the countless unpaid hours they dedicate and the profound emotional labor they undertake – is a crucial step towards creating a more equitable, sustainable, and ultimately, more effective healthcare system for all Australians.

We must move beyond simplistic perceptions and acknowledge the complex reality of a profession that forms the very foundation of our national health.

Today

Yet for my patiients I am
the Doctor of Life.

Chapter 11: What Happens When the GPs Disappear?

The preceding chapters have meticulously outlined the multifaceted pressures currently threatening the viability of General Practice in Australia: chronic underfunding, punitive tax regimes, public misunderstanding, immense workload, and significant emotional toll. While these challenges may seem abstract or primarily affecting the doctors themselves, the ultimate and most devastating consequences of a continued decline in General Practice will be felt directly and profoundly by every single Australian community.

The disappearance – or even a significant reduction in the number and accessibility – of local General Practitioners will trigger a cascade of negative effects that will fundamentally alter the landscape of healthcare access, quality, and cost across the nation. Understanding these dire consequences is crucial to galvanizing the urgent action required to prevent this looming crisis from becoming a devastating reality.

11.1 Reduced Access to Primary Care:

The most immediate and obvious consequence of a GP shortage is a significant reduction in access to timely and affordable primary medical care. This will manifest in several ways:
* Longer Waiting Times: Patients will face increasingly lengthy delays in securing appointments with their local GP, even for urgent but non-emergency medical issues. What was once a wait of a few days might stretch to weeks or even months.
* Fewer Bulk-Billing Clinics: As financial pressures mount, more and more clinics will be forced to abandon bulk-billing altogether or significantly reduce the number of bulk-billed appointments available, placing a greater financial burden on patients, particularly those with lower incomes or chronic health conditions.

* Clinic Closures: As dedicated GPs retire or leave the profession and fewer new doctors choose to enter General Practice, many existing clinics, particularly in rural and outer suburban areas where financial margins are already thin, will be forced to permanently close their doors, leaving entire communities without a local GP.

* Geographic Disparities: The existing maldistribution of GPs, with rural and remote areas already facing significant shortages, will be further exacerbated, creating healthcare deserts where access to even basic primary care becomes a major challenge.

Example – The Rural GP Crisis:
Many small rural towns across Australia are already facing the stark reality of having no local GP or only one or two overworked doctors struggling to serve the entire community. When these doctors retire or move away, finding replacements becomes incredibly difficult, leaving vulnerable populations with severely limited access to essential medical care. This can lead to delayed diagnoses, poorer management of chronic conditions, and an increased reliance on already stretched emergency services located often hundreds of kilometers away.

11.2 Increased Strain on Hospital Emergency Departments:

When access to timely and affordable GP care diminishes, individuals with non-emergency medical conditions will increasingly turn to already overburdened hospital emergency departments (EDs) as their only viable option for seeking medical attention. This will lead to:

* Longer ED Waiting Times: EDs, designed to manage acute and life-threatening emergencies, will become clogged with patients presenting with conditions that could have been effectively and efficiently managed by a GP in the community.

* Increased Costs to the Healthcare System: Treating relatively minor illnesses in an ED setting is significantly more expensive than managing them in a GP clinic. This shift in healthcare utilization will lead to a substantial and unsustainable increase in overall healthcare costs for taxpayers.

* Reduced Quality of Emergency Care: Overcrowded EDs and stretched emergency staff will inevitably lead to a reduction in the quality and timeliness of care for genuinely critical and life-threatening emergencies.

11.3 Poorer Management of Chronic Diseases:

General Practitioners play a crucial role in the ongoing management of chronic diseases such as diabetes, heart disease, asthma, and mental health conditions.

Regular monitoring, medication management, lifestyle advice, and early intervention by a GP are essential for preventing disease progression, reducing complications, and improving patients' quality of life.
When access to GPs is limited:
* Delayed Diagnosis: Early signs and symptoms of chronic diseases may go unnoticed or be dismissed, leading to delayed diagnosis and poorer long-term outcomes.

* Worsening of Existing Conditions: Patients with established chronic diseases may struggle to access regular follow-up appointments, leading to inadequate management of their conditions, increased risk of acute exacerbations, and more frequent hospital admissions.

* Reduced Focus on Preventative Care: Overburdened GPs with less time per patient will have less capacity to focus on preventative health measures, such as screening tests, vaccinations, and lifestyle advice, potentially leading to higher rates of preventable illnesses in the future.

11.4 Decline in Preventative Health and Public Health Outcomes:

General Practitioners are at the forefront of delivering essential preventative health services, including immunizations, cancer screenings, and health education. A decline in GP numbers and accessibility will inevitably lead to:

* Lower Immunization Rates: Reduced access to GPs will make it more difficult for families to ensure their children receive timely and complete immunizations, increasing the risk of outbreaks of preventable infectious diseases within communities.
* Decreased Participation in Screening Programs: Fewer GP appointments will likely lead to lower participation rates in vital cancer screening programs, such as mammography, cervical screening, and bowel cancer screening, potentially resulting in later diagnoses and poorer survival rates.

* Reduced Public Health Surveillance: GPs play a crucial role in identifying and reporting emerging infectious diseases and other public health concerns within their communities. A strained and under-resourced GP workforce will have less capacity for this essential surveillance work, potentially hindering early detection and response to public health threats.

11.5 Erosion of Continuity of Care and Trust:

The long-term relationship between a patient and their regular GP is a cornerstone of high-quality primary care. This continuity of care fosters trust, allows for a deeper understanding of the patient's medical history and individual needs, and leads to better health outcomes.

When patients are forced to see different doctors each time they need care due to GP shortages or clinic closures, this crucial continuity is lost, leading to:

* Fragmented Care: Patients may receive disjointed and uncoordinated care from multiple different doctors who are unfamiliar with their complete medical history.

* Increased Risk of Medical Errors: Lack of continuity can increase the risk of miscommunication, medication errors, and duplication of tests.
* Reduced Patient Satisfaction: Patients often value having a regular GP they know and trust. Losing this relationship can lead to feelings of frustration, anxiety, and dissatisfaction with the healthcare system.

11.6 Economic Impacts on Communities:

The disappearance of GPs can also have significant economic consequences for local communities, particularly in rural and regional areas:

* Loss of Local Businesses: Medical clinics are often significant employers in smaller towns. Clinic closures can lead to job losses for nurses, receptionists, and other support staff, further impacting the local economy.

* Reduced Attractiveness for Residents: Communities without adequate access to healthcare may become less attractive for families and businesses to relocate to, potentially leading to population decline and further economic hardship.

* Increased Costs for Businesses: Businesses may face increased absenteeism and reduced productivity if their employees struggle to access timely medical care.

The Future We Must Avoid:
The scenario outlined above is not a dystopian fantasy; it is a very real and increasingly likely future if the current trajectory of neglect and underfunding of General Practice continues unchecked. The disappearance of GPs will not just be an inconvenience; it will fundamentally undermine the health and well-being of the entire nation, leading to a more expensive, less equitable, and ultimately, sicker Australia.

The time to act is now. We must recognize the critical importance of General Practice as the foundation of our healthcare system and demand urgent and meaningful investment and reform to support these dedicated doctors and ensure that all Australians have access to the high-quality primary care they deserve.

The alternative is a future where healthcare access becomes a postcode lottery, where preventable illnesses overwhelm our hospitals, and where the health and well-being of our communities are severely compromised. The cost of inaction is simply too high to bear.

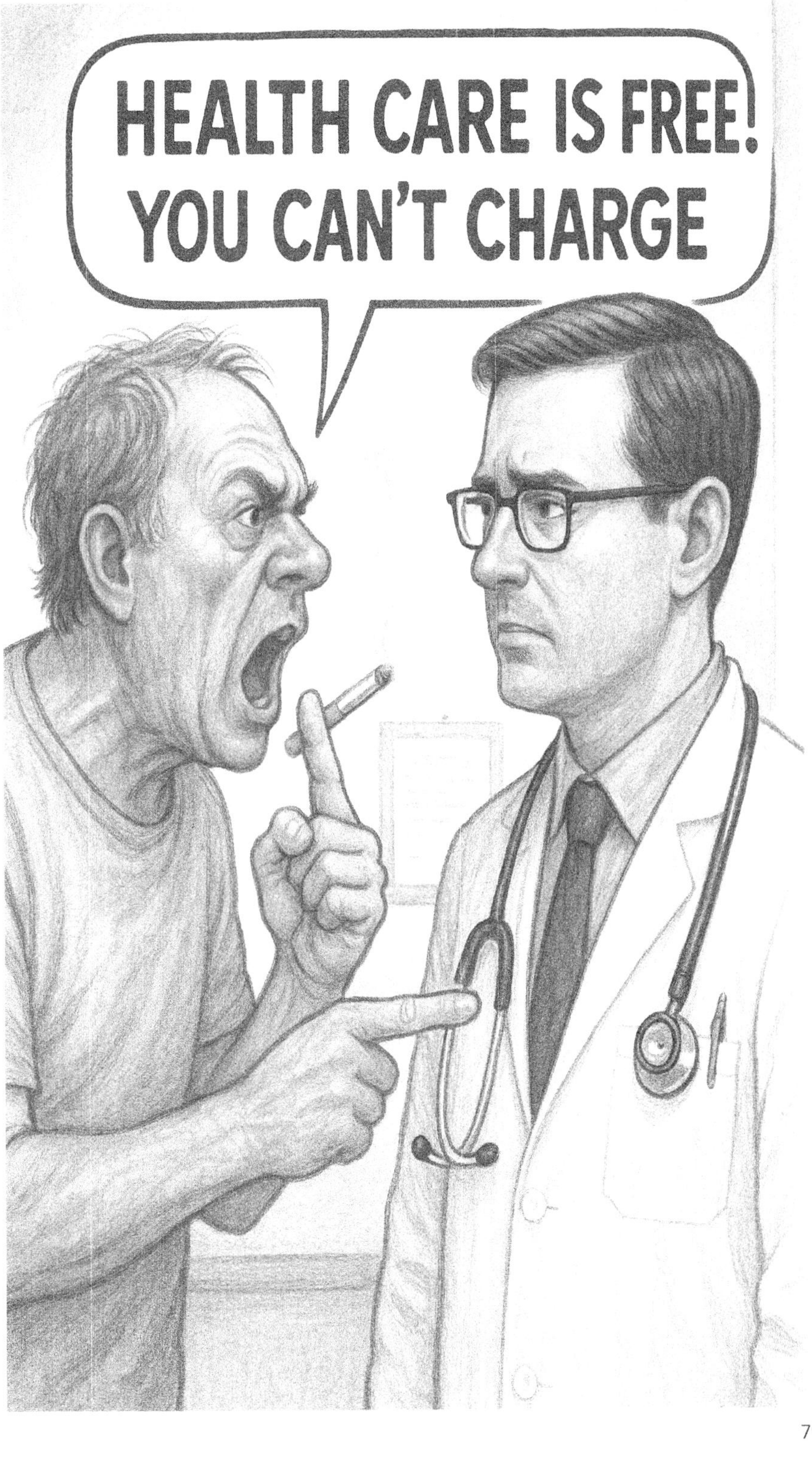
HEALTH CARE IS FREE!
YOU CAN'T CHARGE

Chapter 12: The Hidden Abuse: When Patients Cross the Line

While the focus of this book has rightly been on the systemic pressures and challenges facing General Practitioners, it is also crucial to acknowledge a difficult and often unspoken aspect of their daily reality: the increasing prevalence of verbal abuse, aggressive behavior, and a sense of entitlement exhibited by a small but significant minority of patients.

This is not to excuse or diminish the genuine frustrations that many patients experience when navigating an increasingly strained healthcare system. However, there is a growing trend of unacceptable behavior directed towards frontline healthcare workers, including GPs and their staff, which contributes significantly to stress, burnout, and a feeling of being unsafe in their own workplaces.

The Spectrum of Unacceptable Behavior:

The types of abusive behavior encountered by GPs and their staff can range from:

* Verbal Aggression: Shouting, swearing, insults, and condescending language directed at doctors and reception staff.

* Unrealistic Demands: Insistent and often aggressive demands for immediate appointments, specific medications, or referrals that may not be clinically appropriate or feasible.

* Threatening Behavior: Overt or implied threats of violence, complaints to regulatory bodies based on unreasonable expectations, or online harassment and defamation.

* Entitlement and Disrespect: A sense of entitlement to immediate and unconditional service, a lack of respect for the doctor's time and expertise, and a refusal to accept reasonable explanations or limitations.

* Physical Aggression (Rare but Serious): While thankfully less common, instances of physical intimidation or violence against healthcare workers do occur and represent a serious safety concern.

The Contributing Factors:
Several factors may contribute to this concerning trend:

* Increased Patient Frustration: As access to timely and affordable healthcare becomes more challenging, some patients understandably feel frustrated and may direct their anger and frustration towards the frontline staff they interact with.

* Misinformation and Entitlement: Misleading media portrayals of GPs as highly paid or the misconception of a completely "free" healthcare system can fuel unrealistic expectations and a sense of entitlement.

* Stress and Anxiety: Patients dealing with illness, pain, or anxiety may be more prone to irritability and aggressive behavior.

* Mental Health Issues and Substance Abuse: In some cases, underlying mental health conditions or substance abuse may contribute to aggressive or inappropriate behavior.
* Erosion of Trust: The constant negative portrayal of doctors in some media outlets and by some politicians can erode public trust and respect for the profession.

The Impact on GPs and Their Staff:

Experiencing patient abuse, even verbal, can have a significant and detrimental impact on the well-being of General Practitioners and their dedicated staff:

* Increased Stress and Anxiety: Facing aggressive or entitled behavior can be highly stressful and contribute to feelings of anxiety and fear in the workplace.

* Burnout and Compassion Fatigue: Constant exposure to negativity and disrespect can erode empathy and increase the risk of burnout and compassion fatigue.

* Reduced Job Satisfaction: Feeling unsafe or unappreciated in their workplace can significantly reduce job satisfaction and contribute to doctors and staff leaving the profession.

* Impact on Patient Care: When doctors and staff are feeling stressed or intimidated, their ability to provide compassionate and effective care may be compromised.

* Safety Concerns: In the rare but serious cases of physical aggression or threats, the safety of healthcare workers is directly at risk.

The Need for a Culture of Respect:

While GPs and their staff are dedicated to providing care to all patients, it is crucial to foster a culture of mutual respect and understanding within the healthcare setting. Unacceptable behavior should not be tolerated, and medical practices have a right to implement policies to protect their staff and ensure a safe working environment.

This includes:
* Clear Communication: Practices should clearly communicate their appointment policies, billing practices, and expectations of patient behavior.

* De-escalation Strategies: Staff should be trained in de-escalation techniques to manage difficult patient interactions.

* Support for Staff: Practices should provide support and resources for staff who have experienced patient abuse.

* Zero Tolerance Policies: Clear policies outlining unacceptable behavior and the consequences of such behavior should be implemented and enforced.

* Public Education: Efforts are needed to educate the public about the pressures facing the healthcare system and the importance of treating healthcare workers with respect.

The vast majority of patients are grateful for the care they receive from their General Practitioners. However, the actions of a small minority can have a significant and negative impact on the well-being of those who dedicate their lives to caring for others. A healthy healthcare system requires not only adequate funding and supportive policies but also a culture of mutual respect and understanding between patients and their healthcare providers.

Chapter 13: Doctor of Life

"There's a unique rhythm to a day in general practice. It's a demanding rhythm, a constant ebb and flow of human stories, of medical puzzles, of moments of quiet triumph and deep concern. We navigate the complexities of illness, the fragility of life, and the resilience of the human spirit. It can be exhausting, yes, but it's also a source of profound meaning. Even amidst the challenges, there's a current of hope that runs through it all, a sense of purpose that sustains us.
I often find myself reflecting on this duality – the weight and the wonder, the struggle and the privilege. We are privileged to be invited into the lives of our patients, to share their journeys, to offer comfort and healing. And in those moments of reflection, when I try to capture the essence of what it means to be a GP, it often comes out in words like

Doctor of life, Poem.

Today,
I look to my left and right
There is no colleague by my side—
No nurse, registrar, RMO or intern for support.
I do the obs, write the notes, and look after patients by myself.

Today,
I do a neonatal check, treat scabies.
Support the mum with postnatal depression.
Address the concerns of a child-health nurse for a child with failure to thrive.
Refer to the paediatrician for ADHD review because a teacher reached out to me.

Today,
I do a few skin checks, cut out some lesions, and do some dressing.
I chase a few results my ED colleague asked me to, and change medications per the physician's advice.
I arrange patient-travel because the specialist forgot.

Today,
I do CBT for my patient with severe depression.
I counsel my crying 87-year-old who lost her husband of 60 years.
My heart breaks a little, but I keep going
Before I click the next patient, I wipe my tears for a minute.

Today,
I am shouted at by a drug-seeker.
I apply for a stimulant permit because my psychiatrist colleague is too busy.
I de-escalate complaints about my colleague from hospital.

Today,
I assess suicide risk for one patient and create advance-care plans for another.
I bulk-bill a few who struggle with addiction, depression, grief.

Happy to give care even though I earn less for my family this week.

As you say, I am "just a GP."
Yet for my patients I am the Doctor of Life.

This is a snapshot – a fleeting glimpse into the daily life of a General Practitioner. It is a life lived in service, a constant juggling act of medical knowledge, emotional support, and administrative demands, all within the constraints of a system that often feels like it is working against them. They are the doctors of life, witnessing its full spectrum, one consultation at a time.

Final Chapter: The Six-Minute Myth and the Future of Care

The persistent myth of the "$400k GP" stands in stark and brutal contrast to the lived reality of a profession increasingly defined by six-minute consultations, a desperate attempt to maintain financial viability within a chronically underfunded system.

This fundamental disconnect – between the inflated public perception of GP wealth and the daily struggle to provide quality care within unsustainable timeframes – lies at the very heart of the crisis engulfing Australian primary care.

The economic pressure created by stagnant Medicare rebates and punitive tax regimes forces many dedicated GPs into a relentless treadmill of short consultations. The sheer volume of patients they must see each day to keep their practices afloat leaves precious little time for the nuanced history-taking, thorough examination, thoughtful consideration of complex medical issues, and crucial patient education that truly effective primary care demands.

The Erosion of Quality and Compassion:

When consultations are reduced to a rushed six-minute transaction, the quality of care inevitably suffers:

* Superficial Assessments: GPs are forced to make rapid assessments based on limited information, increasing the risk of missed diagnoses or inadequate management plans.

* Limited Patient Education: There is insufficient time to properly explain medical conditions, treatment options, or preventative health strategies, leaving patients feeling confused and disempowered.

* Reduced Empathy and Connection: The rushed nature of consultations can erode the vital therapeutic relationship between doctor and patient, leading to feelings of being unheard and uncared for.

* Increased Risk of Burnout: The constant pressure to churn through patients at an unsustainable pace contributes significantly to GP burnout and reduces job satisfaction.

The False Economy of Short Consultations

While short consultations may appear to be a cost-saving measure in the short term, they ultimately lead to a false economy with significant long-term consequences:

* Delayed Diagnoses: Subtle or complex conditions may be missed in rushed consultations, leading to delayed diagnoses and potentially more serious and costly health problems down the line.

* Poorer Chronic Disease Management: Inadequate time for comprehensive chronic disease management can lead to poorer health outcomes, increased complications, and more frequent hospital admissions.

* Increased Hospitalizations: When primary care fails to effectively manage conditions in the community, more patients will inevitably require more expensive hospital-based care.
* Reduced Focus on Prevention: The lack of time for preventative health discussions will contribute to higher rates of preventable illnesses in the future, further straining the healthcare system.

The Future of Care: A Choice We Must Make

The current trajectory of underfunding and the resulting pressure for ever-shorter consultations represent a dangerous race to the bottom for Australian primary care.

We stand at a critical juncture where we must make a fundamental choice about the future of our healthcare system:

* Continue down the path of prioritizing short-term cost savings at the expense of quality, compassion, and the long-term health of our communities?

This path leads to a system where GPs are increasingly burnt out and disillusioned, where access to comprehensive primary care becomes a luxury, and where the burden on our already strained hospitals becomes unbearable.

* Or, make a conscious and significant reinvestment in General Practice, recognizing its fundamental importance as the bedrock of a sustainable and equitable healthcare system?

This path requires a commitment to increasing Medicare rebates to reflect the true cost of delivering high-quality care, supporting longer and more comprehensive consultations, and valuing the expertise and dedication of our General Practitioners.

The six-minute consultation is not a sustainable model for the future of primary care. It is a symptom of a system starved of the resources it needs to function effectively. To truly heal our healthcare system, we must move beyond the damaging myths and embrace the reality that quality primary care requires time, expertise, and adequate funding.

The future of care in Australia depends on the choices we make today. Will we continue to prioritize a false economy of speed and superficiality, or will we invest in a system that values the health and well-being of both patients and the dedicated doctors who care for them?

The answer to this question will determine the health of our nation for generations to come.

Appendix 1: Locum GP Rates – The Exception, Not the Rule.

A common retort when discussing the financial pressures faced by General Practitioners is the seemingly high hourly rates advertised for locum (temporary) GP positions.

While it is true that locum rates can appear attractive on the surface, it is crucial to understand that these rates represent a fundamentally different employment model and do not accurately reflect the income or financial security of the vast majority of permanent GPs.

Several key factors contribute to the higher hourly rates for locum work:

* Lack of Job Security: Locum positions are inherently temporary, often lasting only a few days or weeks. Locums have no guarantee of ongoing work and face significant income uncertainty between placements.

* No Employment Benefits: Locums typically receive none of the standard employment benefits that salaried doctors in hospitals often enjoy, such as paid sick leave, paid annual leave, employer-funded superannuation, or long service leave. They are solely responsible for covering these costs themselves.

* High Overhead Costs: Locums often incur significant travel and accommodation expenses to work in different locations, further reducing their net income. They are also responsible for their own medical indemnity insurance and professional registration fees.
* Addressing Workforce Shortages: High locum rates are often a reflection of the desperate need to fill temporary staffing gaps, particularly in rural and remote areas or during peak demand periods. They are a symptom of the underlying GP shortage, not an indication of widespread high earnings within the profession.

* No Continuity of Care Responsibility: Locums typically do not have the ongoing responsibility for managing complex chronic conditions or

providing continuity of care for a regular patient base, which is a significant component of a permanent GP's workload and requires substantial unpaid time for tasks like reviewing patient histories and coordinating care plans.

Therefore, while a locum GP might earn a seemingly high hourly rate, their overall annual income, job security, and access to benefits are often significantly lower than those of a permanent GP working consistent hours. Furthermore, the high cost of locum coverage places an additional financial strain on medical practices, further highlighting the inadequacy of current Medicare funding.

Focusing solely on locum rates as an indicator of GP earnings provides a distorted and incomplete picture of the true financial realities faced by the vast majority of dedicated General Practitioners who are committed to providing continuous and comprehensive care to their communities.

Locum work is an essential part of the healthcare system, particularly in filling temporary gaps, but it is the exception, not the rule, and its higher rates reflect the inherent instability and lack of benefits associated with temporary employment.

Google
REVIEWS
Saying bad things
on internet and
abusing GP

Appendix 2: Stories That Keep Us Going

Responding to
"If You're So Unhappy, Why Don't You Just Quit?"
"Rich people crying for more money!!! What kind of doctor are you !!!"
"You can't charge me , I am calling Medicare to report you!!! "
"Why MRI charge ?"
"Why I need to pay for travel vaccines ?"
"Last doctor just sign for me , if you don't sign , I call APRHA and report you!"

A frustrating and often dismissive comment directed towards General Practitioners who voice concerns about the pressures and challenges of their profession is: "If you're so unhappy, why don't you just quit?"

This sentiment, while perhaps understandable from individuals unfamiliar with the deep commitment and sense of responsibility that drives most GPs, fundamentally misunderstands the complex factors at play. Quitting is rarely a simple or desirable solution for dedicated doctors who are deeply invested in the well-being of their patients and their communities.

Here are several key reasons why "just quitting" is not the easy answer it may seem:

* Deep Sense of Vocation: The vast majority of GPs chose this demanding profession because they genuinely care about helping people and making a positive difference in their communities. This sense of vocation and commitment to their patients runs deep, making the thought of abandoning their responsibilities incredibly difficult.

* Responsibility for Patient Care: GPs often have long-standing relationships with their patients, some spanning decades. They feel a profound sense of responsibility for their ongoing care and worry about the impact their departure would have on their health and well-being, particularly for those with complex or chronic conditions.

* Moral and Ethical Obligations: Doctors take an oath to care for their patients. Leaving a community without adequate medical care can feel like a breach of that ethical obligation.
* Significant Investment in Training: Becoming a specialist General Practitioner requires over a decade of rigorous education and training. Walking away from this significant investment is a difficult decision, both personally and professionally.

* Limited Alternative Options: While some GPs may consider specializing in a different field, this often requires further extensive training and may not align with their passion for comprehensive primary care. Leaving medicine altogether represents a drastic career change after years of dedicated study and practice.

* Fear for the Future of Primary Care: Many GPs are deeply concerned about the future of primary care in Australia and feel a responsibility to stay and fight for the necessary changes to ensure its survival for future generations. Quitting can feel like abandoning that fight.

* The System Needs Fixing, Not Abandonment: The issues highlighted in this book are systemic problems requiring systemic solutions. Individual GPs leaving the profession, while understandable in some cases, does not address the fundamental flaws in funding, policy, and public perception that are driving the crisis.

While burnout and disillusionment are sadly leading some GPs to leave the profession, the vast majority remain deeply committed to their patients and their communities. Their advocacy for change is not a sign of weakness or a reason to simply quit; it is a passionate plea to fix a broken system so that they can continue to provide the high-quality care that Australians deserve, without sacrificing their own well-being in the process.

The answer lies not in GPs quitting, but in the community and policymakers recognizing the critical importance of their role and taking urgent action to support them.

More Real Stories of Connection and Warmth (Names Diverted)

Amidst the systemic challenges and the often-heavy emotional burdens, the daily life of a General Practitioner is also punctuated by moments of genuine warmth, unexpected kindness, and the profound feeling of being deeply connected to their community.

These interactions, often small and seemingly insignificant, serve as vital reminders of the human element at the heart of medicine and the unique privilege of being a trusted part of people's lives.

Dr. Liam O'Connell still smiles when he remembers old Mr. Henderson, a stoic farmer who rarely showed much emotion. After Liam successfully diagnosed and treated a rare infection that had baffled other doctors, Mr. Henderson, on his next visit, presented him with a carefully chosen selection of his prize-winning tomatoes, each one gleaming red and perfectly ripe. "They're the best of the season, son," he'd grunted, a rare hint of a smile playing on his lips. "A small thanks for sorting me out." Liam shared them with his family that evening, a tangible reminder of the impact of his work.

Then there was young Maya, a shy eight-year-old who had struggled with selective mutism. Dr. O'Connell had worked patiently with her and her family for months, building trust and slowly encouraging her to communicate. One day, while Liam was walking through the local park on his day off, he heard a small, clear voice call out, "Hello, Dr. Liam!" Maya, swinging on the monkey bars, beamed at him, her newfound confidence radiating. It was a simple greeting, but it represented a significant victory and a deeply moving moment.

Dr. Aisha Khan keeps a colourful, slightly crumpled card pinned above her desk. It was created by the entire Peterson family after she helped their teenage son navigate a severe mental health crisis. The card, filled with drawings of sunshine and rainbows and handwritten messages of gratitude from each family member, serves as a constant reminder of the profound trust they placed in her during a very difficult time.

One busy afternoon, an elderly lady, Mrs. Yamamoto, who spoke limited English, tried to discreetly slip a twenty-dollar note into Dr. Khan's hand after she carefully explained her new medication regimen. Despite Dr. Khan's gentle refusal, Mrs. Yamamoto kept gesturing towards it with a grateful expression. Understanding the cultural significance of showing appreciation in this way, Dr. Khan suggested she should use the money to buy a small plant for the clinic waiting room, a gesture that brought a warm smile to her face and benefited everyone.

For Dr. Ben Rossi, his practice felt like an extension of his own family. He had been the GP for the entire Nguyen clan since he first started his career, delivering their grandchildren and supporting them through various health scares and milestones. It wasn't unusual for Mrs. Nguyen to bring in a large container of her delicious spring rolls for the clinic staff or for him to receive a flurry of enthusiastic "Hi, Dr. Ben!" greetings from the Nguyen children whenever he saw them around town. He felt deeply embedded in their lives.

These authentic moments – the gift of homegrown produce, a child's breakthrough in communication, a family's heartfelt card, a culturally significant offering of thanks, the feeling of being a trusted family friend – are the quiet joys that often sustain General Practitioners through the long hours and emotional demands of their profession.

They highlight the deep human connections forged within the community and the profound impact they have on individual lives. These are the real stories that underscore the enduring rewards of a career dedicated to caring for others.

Final Reflection: Building Bridges, Not Divisions

The crisis in Australian General Practice is not a battle between doctors and patients, or between the profession and the government. It is a shared challenge that demands a collaborative and compassionate response from all stakeholders.

The dedicated General Practitioners of Australia are not asking for exorbitant wealth or an easy life. They are asking for fair recognition of their expertise, adequate funding for the essential services they provide, and a sustainable system that allows them to deliver high-quality, comprehensive care without sacrificing their own well-being.
The health of our nation is inextricably linked to the health of our primary care system.

When GPs are supported and valued, patients benefit from better access, improved continuity of care, and ultimately, better health outcomes. When the foundation of our healthcare system crumbles, the entire structure is at risk of collapse.

Let us move beyond the damaging myths and the divisive rhetoric. Let us build bridges of understanding and work together – patients, doctors, policymakers, and the media – to ensure a vibrant and sustainable future for General Practice in Australia. The time for blame is over. The time for action is now. The health of our communities depends on it.

Conclusion: A Shared Future!

The stories and realities shared within these pages paint a clear and urgent picture. Australian General Practice, the bedrock of our healthcare system, is facing an unprecedented crisis. Chronic underfunding, punitive policies, public misunderstanding, and the sheer weight of unsustainable workloads are pushing dedicated doctors to their limits, threatening the very accessibility and quality of primary care that all Australians deserve.

This is not a problem that will resolve itself. It demands our collective attention, our empathy, and our unwavering commitment to finding meaningful solutions. The myths and misinformation that have clouded the public discourse must be dispelled by the clear light of truth and understanding. We must recognize the profound value of General Practitioners – their extensive training, their crucial role in our communities, and the immense responsibility they carry each and every day.

The small acts of kindness and the deep connections forged between GPs and their patients, while heartwarming and sustaining, cannot alone solve the systemic issues at hand. We need policy changes that reflect the true cost of delivering high-quality primary care. We need funding models that prioritize patient well-being and the sustainability of medical practices over short-sighted cost-cutting measures. We need a public that understands and values the vital role of their family doctors.

The future of Australian healthcare is a shared responsibility. It requires open and honest conversations, a willingness to challenge long-held assumptions, and a unified commitment to building a system that supports both patients and the dedicated professionals who care for them. The time for complacency is over. The time for action is now. Let us work together to ensure a healthy and sustainable future for General Practice, and for the health of our nation.

The End

The Art of Healing

The art of healing
is more than the stitch,
the cut and suture,
the blood and bone.
It is listening with warmed hands
and open eyes.
It is the heart that heals
It is the grace
Let in when a door is left ajar.

...

There are myriad paths leading to station 21
Along the journey, we all confront our fears
Do your burdens weigh too heavily upon you?
Do not relinquish hope, your Savior manifests
Steadfastly pursue the mission
Find solace upon the cornerstone
A healing balm shall envelop the spirit
Until we traverse hand in hand towards home.

...

Made in United States
Orlando, FL
12 July 2025